This book is my recollection of the 18 years
I spent living at Lentz Mortuary.
The events described are true in their entirety.

IF THESE WALLS COULD SPEAK,

THE UNDERTAKER'S DAUGHTER
An Autobiography

Ina Lentz Griesbeck

*In loving memory of the
undertaker, my mother,
Winter Hawk, all of those
in the nether world,
and all of those who
crossed over.*

Copyright © 2010 Ina Lentz Griesbeck

All rights reserved. No part of this book may be used or reproduced in any manner whatsoever without written permission except in the case of brief quotations embodied in critical articles and reviews.

ISBN 978-0-61539437-4

Printed in the United States of America

First Printing September 2010

CONTENTS

Introduction by Ina Lentz Griesbeck	7
Chapter 1: Lentz Mortuary, Raeford, N.C.	11
Chapter 2: Life – and Death – at Lentz Mortuary	21
Chapter 3: Two Women, Two Murders and a Bird	27
Chapter 4: Buried Memories	37
Chapter 5: Runaway Hearse	45
Chapter 6: Holidays at Lentz Mortuary	51
Chapter 7: Phyllis and the Others	61
Chapter 8: Devastating Descent	75
Chapter 9: No Medical Explanation	83
Chapter 10: A Gruesome Education	87
Chapter 11: High School Hijinks	93
Chapter 12: Winter Hawk Hell	99
Chapter 13: Violent Consequences	109
Chapter 14: Starting Over	119
Chapter 15: Confirmation at Last	125
Chapter 16: The Undertaker's Funeral	129
Chapter 17: Keys to a New Life	135
Last Words….	138
Acknowledgements	139
What Everyone Should Know About Autism	141

INTRODUCTION

It's been more than 40 years, but I remember every detail of the door that led to the embalming room in our basement.

The paint was old, chipped and no longer white. The door had clearly stood the test of time, but despite its deteriorating appearance, it managed to maintain a sort of refined dignity. It had character that was evident in the round, glass doorknob that would forever remind me of a gypsy's crystal ball.

The doorknob mesmerized me, and as a young child I would stare into the glass knob for hours, always with the feeling that something or someone was calling to me from behind that door. I remember sitting and gazing, waiting for a mystery to be revealed.

But I dared not open that captivating door. My father had the only key – an aptly named, old-fashioned skeleton key.

Most kids grow up with the smell of fresh-baked cookies coming from the oven. I grew up in a funeral home – surrounded by very different smells and echoing sounds that often kept other kids away.

A very distinct sound, like a screaming train whistle, reverberated through the house when my father, the undertaker, opened that weathered door. As the door opened and the train thundered past, it brought the overpowering and inescapable scent of death. My father, the undertaker, was, in effect, the conductor who released it into the air every time he opened that door. The scent of death can be neither described nor forgotten, and once you have encountered it, you will always recognize it for what it is, and for what it is not – life.

We do not choose our parents or the circumstances into which we are born. But is it possible perhaps those circumstances might choose us? I am open to the possibility that this house chose me.

I entered the world as Ina Elizabeth Lentz in April 1963 and was an only child, named after my father's mother, who died right around my first birthday.

The three of us lived at 411 West Prospect Ave., Raeford, N.C., but I would soon discover that I was not the only child who called the place home. The address was that of Lentz Mortuary and it was my home for 18 years. I was the undertaker's daughter.

My father died on Christmas in 2000. Shortly after his death, I came across an old wooden box that had belonged to him. As I opened it, a familiar presence surrounded me – a presence I once felt as a little girl.

The box held a collection of skeleton keys and the clear glass doorknob that when turned, released the scent of death in our home.

I suppose the undertaker accumulated all the skeleton keys much like he acquired skeletons in his closet. Only now, they live in mine, and I write this to set them free.

CHAPTER 1

Lentz Mortuary, Raeford, N.C.

Raeford, North Carolina is a small town of back roads and front porches. It's about 55 miles west of Interstate 95, and in the 1960s it was governed by Southern traditions. Raeford folks exuded warm hospitality, old-fashioned manners and a general sense of contentment that comes from a slow pace of life. Of course, there was the same class division that marked every American town in the tumultuous 60s, but most of the children attended the same school.

My dad bought the three-story, white-shingled house on West Prospect Avenue in the 1947. Green shutters defined the front windows of the old structure that my father would convert into a funeral home.

He bought the contents of the old defunct MacDiarmid Funeral Home, and according to Raeford locals, moved everything by himself. He refused help from anyone, and folks still wonder how he moved all those old wooden caskets, boxes and crates. Some say he rigged up a pulley, but he was very secretive about what he was doing, and the project remains a bit of a small-town mystery.

The laws were different back in the 1950s, and there were fewer regulations about the operation of a funeral home.

The undertaker was proud of his enterprise, and a wooden white sign declaring "Lentz Mortuary" hung from an old wooden pole in front of the house next to the road. When the wind blew, the sign would sway and squeak as if trying to get someone's attention.

The driveway was circular in front of the funeral home. A small, wooden door, about 5½ feet high, was located in the back of the house. The door was intriguingly small and led to the basement of our house, the funeral home.

The basement and its accompanying embalming room were off limits to me for as long as I could remember. An old interior staircase rose from the basement to the first floor of our house, and it echoed with every creaking step someone took. A door at the top of the steep staircase led into the funeral home. It was the knob on this door that hypnotized me for hours as a child. Little did I know how many secrets it would someday reveal.

Most days found me playing in the woods around our house. They separated our house from the home of Elwood and Freddy Cox, who lived behind us.

A grapevine at the Cox house grew so thick that not even sunlight could penetrate. I spent many warm, summer afternoons, sneaking over and eating as many grapes as my little stomach would hold. I would carry them in my shirt along a path that was created over the years between the invasive wild vines that stretched as far as the eye could see and created a jungle between the neighboring properties.

Younger Snead owned the thickly wooded lot next to our house. His wife taught school and awaited my arrival in the world of first grade. No vines grew in the Sneads' woodsy thicket that was filled with cedar and pine trees, but it was filled with wild blackberries that I picked in season. Blackberries with milk and sugar were a favorite summer treat. The outskirts of the woods were also the best spot to catch fireflies. I always used an empty Duke's mayonnaise jar to construct myself a firefly lantern. The lids were sturdy enough to withstand the air holes I created with an old ice pick.

As a young child I was only allowed to play within a designated area, but in those days it was common for children to play outside with only occasional supervision from a mother glancing out a window. Even though Raeford was considered a town, it was not unusual for folks to sleep at night with only a screen door locked.

I was about four years old when I saw my daddy, the undertaker, getting out of his customized, black station wagon in the backyard. There was a big door in the back of the car with a wide, curtained window. The undertaker's station wagon was different from any other car I had seen. The front seat was made of red leather, and there were two doors on each side with deep vertical windows. My last name, Lentz, was proudly displayed on removable name plates between the draped silver curtains. As a little girl, it was easy for me to learn to spell my last name, as it was always visible on our car. My first name is the one that would give me spelling trouble.

As the car pulled into the backyard, I remember peeking through the bushes to see what was going on. The undertaker was hollering for my mother while opening the back door to the oversized station wagon. The mysterious cargo was obviously heavy, prompting my father to utter several obscene words under his breath. My mother had maneuvered her way to the back of the wagon until both were using obscene words, and my mother was never one to use profanity. They emerged from the car carrying a long object on an unusual table with handles. There was an off-white sheet draped over the mystery cargo. The undertaker lifted one end while my mother carried the other from the station wagon toward the wooden door leading to the basement.

I ran from the yard to the basement window, and tried to get a glimpse through the old cracked windows, but could see only darkness on the other side. That window was forever dark, and no one could ever see what took place on the other side.

Whatever my parents had carried into the basement gave

me a feeling of immediate uneasiness. It was a stifling hot summer day but I still remember the chills that ran down my spine.

Of course I eventually learned that the undertaker's black station wagon was a hearse. The weight that the undertaker and his wife carried was a dead body on a stretcher draped with a ghostly white sheet.

My daddy the undertaker was a mysterious man of many talents, and that made him popular among the townsfolk. He opened an antique store on the outskirts of town, and converted the upstairs area into a flower shop. He knew a lot about the antiques that he sold, and he often had handled the funerals for their former owners. People would drop off their family heirlooms for my father to buy and then resell.

He was respected as a shrewd but fair businessman when it came to antiques.

Raeford newspaper columnist Lilmar Sue Gatlin Williams wrote an article about my father and her memories of Jim Lentz's Antique Shop. It was published in the "News-Journal" in 2010, and alluded to the mysterious unpredictability of my father's moods and reactions.

"The twinkle in his smile carried enough electricity to start a fire," Williams wrote. "The only problem was you never had any idea what it might ignite."

Ms. Williams has no idea how accurately she described my father. Her article goes on to describe one of her family's entertaining experiences at Jim Lentz's Antique Shop.

The writer's great-grandmother was in her 90s when she began worrying that she would outlive her savings. The woman quelled her fears by wandering around her home in search of items she could live without, but that others might want.

Grandmother combed her dining room, parlor and music room and bagged up anything she thought others may want. She had amassed quite a collection of silver, china and crystal by the time she walked the block to my father's shop.

My father bought everything, lock, stock and barrel, and he happily handed Ms. Williams' great-grandmother cash in return for her belongings.

"As Grandmother headed home with a smile on her face, Jim was grabbing the phonebook, grinning as he dialed," Williams wrote.

My father proceeded to call the old woman's relatives, and told them what she had done. The younger women went immediately to the antique shop and bought back every heirloom, not wanting anyone other than family to possess the old treasures. Here was my father making a profit by selling antiques back to the family that would have inherited them, but he was able to convince the customers that he was doing them a favor.

"Knowing Jim he got a great giggle at the profit he made from the sale, and Mother, Aunt Mamie and Aunt Frances were very pleased to have Jim on their side. That's the Jim Lentz charm and you had to have known him to recognize it," she wrote.

In addition to his reputation as a shrewd antiques dealer, my father was also known for his floral masterpieces that honored the dead. It had become part of the ritual for the undertaker to create an arrangement for the individual lying dead in our dining room.

I often helped my father bundle bunches of flowers, and my little fingers would blister from the countless ribbons I attached to green picks.

I was not yet 5 years old when I asked the undertaker what an undertaker does. He said that he worked for our Maker, that he got people ready to meet their Maker so they could cross over to the other side. Apparently it was an insult to cross over wearing anything other than your best Sunday outfit.

Speaking of Sundays, everybody went to church in Raeford. White folks could choose from the Church of God, Methodist, Baptist or Presbyterian, while black people and Indians attended their own churches.

The undertaker was in no way prejudiced when it came to a proper burial. Local town folks always commented on the undertaker's sincerity. It did not matter if you were male or female, black, white or yellow, you could be guaranteed the undertaker would give you a proper burial.

As in most churches, the ones in Raeford provided weekly updates on the latest community news. In addition, you noticed if someone wore the same thing to church two Sundays in a row. Back then the main town event was an annual church picnic. It didn't matter which church you belonged to, you still had a picnic. Usually the minister would always be the judge of the dessert contest, which was my favorite event.

I was a member of Raeford Presbyterian Church and attended Sunday school. Reverend Cooper baptized me but Dr. John C. Ropp was the church minister from the time I was three years old. I always felt special because Reverend Ropp and I shared an April 25 birthday. I imagine some folks thought it was a silly belief but I felt connected to him as a child.

I thought it strange that everyone always sat in the same place at church every Sunday. I knew there wasn't designated seating, but would bet that the people who are still alive are still sitting in those same spots in those same wooden pews.

In addition to knowing their seats in church, everybody also always knew when someone died. It was customary to take food over to the family's home and pay your respects, then sit around and share wonderful stories about the departed. Southern fried chicken, potato salad, collard greens and corn bread were the most popular offerings, along with pies and cakes.

Raeford was a small town with few secrets, and the townspeople took pride in the knowledge they had of everyone's business. But the house at 411 West Prospect Ave. contained more than its share of secrets, and I've often wondered how much anyone in Raeford really knew about what went on behind the closed doors of Lentz Mortuary.

CHAPTER 2
Life – and Death – at Lentz Mortuary

My parents never celebrated their wedding anniversary. I remember hearing other grown-ups talk about anniversary dinners, or flowers that were delivered for a silver anniversary. But the day was not recognized, or even noted on the calendar. My parents' marriage was not something to celebrate.

They got married in 1962 after my mother learned she was pregnant. And though my father, and society, undoubtedly felt he was doing the right and honorable thing, I have to wonder how my life would have turned out if he had left the pregnant, country girl named LaRue Brennan behind.

LaRue came from the poor, rural area of White Oak, N.C., a two-hour drive from Raeford. She grew up with eight siblings that each towered over her, as my mother was just two inches shy of being classified a midget.

The diminutive Miss Brennan was living in Fayetteville and working for the phone company by the time she met the charming and educated Jim Lentz in 1962.

One night of muttered promises and impassioned mistakes led to a life of resentment, violence and resigned acceptance of it all.

Perhaps my mother put up with it all because in her own, inexplicable way, she truly loved my father, and she did anything he demanded of her. She was devoted to this controlling man who resented us both, as we were constant reminders of the life my dad had forfeited by marrying this simple, but devoted country girl.

My father never thought my mother was good enough for him. We just didn't fit into his world, and as if to prove it, there were only two photos ever taken that showed all three of us as a family.

I don't know when my father started beating my mother. But I know I got my first taste of his favorite stout, leather strap – the kind barbers use to sharpen their straight razors – when I was four years old, and tried to tell my father that I saw ghosts in our house.

From then on, he would beat me with that strap every time I tried to tell him what I saw or heard. He beat my mother for other reasons, and used that strap on our backs, butts and legs.

We tried to predict his tantrums, and would hide in the woods near our house to avoid my father and his strap. We often fell asleep in those woods when I was child, and we were waiting out his unpredictable temper. We had no blankets or food, except for the wild grapes on the Cox vines. But the cold and hunger were better than the alternative inside.

My dad was not a drinker, so the source of his anger was a mystery. But it was intense, and I can't imagine the number of beatings my mother endured for me, trying to absorb the worst of his wrath to spare her only child. Some beatings were so severe that my mother could not leave the house for two weeks at a time.

Situations like those make me wonder how much the rest of the town knew, or assumed, about life at Lentz Mortuary, and why no one bothered to ask if things were OK. Then again, my father was a pillar of the community. He made sure that poor people were properly buried, and were respected in death. He embalmed and buried black people as well as white despite racial clashes in North Carolina in the 60s. He offered steadfast comfort to grieving widows, heartbroken husbands and orphaned children. No one dared mention that all might not be well behind closed doors and darkened windows.

But once the violence ended, my father usually left the house. He rarely slept with his family in the funeral home, but preferred to stay in an apartment he kept at the antique shop. My father led a separate life at night, but he and I spent our days together before I started school. The beatings were most severe when I mentioned the ghosts that I saw, so I learned at an early age to keep quiet about such inexplicable things that no one else apparently saw.

I had started hearing "the others" when I was only 3. The first experience sounded like three or four people were sharing a secret in our living room on Christmas Eve, but there was no one else in the room. Those sounds and voices developed into clearer visions by the time I was four.

My Godmother Eloise was the first person I saw cross over to the other world. She had lived in Raeford all her life, and had died in her sleep at age 72, entrusting her funeral arrangements to my father, the town's deeply trusted and highly respected undertaker.

Godmother Eloise was laid out in her casket in the funeral home parlor, when I saw her rise up from that shiny, bronze casket into a standing position. She was no longer human, but rather appeared nearly transparent, but still smiling her friendly smile. She no longer wore glasses, and I seemed to watch the aging process reverse. The gray left her hair, and her wrinkles had disappeared, leaving smooth skin on a beautiful face.

I only saw her for a few seconds. While the transformation occurred, I developed an internal alert. I immediately got butterfulies in my stomach which became a sign when someone crossed over, those butterflies would revisit me time and time again. Regardless of where I was, as each soul ceased to exist in our known world, I was made aware.

I had always known there was a higher power in the universe because of all the souls I saw cross over. The church people referred to that power as God. My father called him our Maker. I called him the Creator and still do.

In addition to our Creator, I also always knew that ghosts lived among us. Some were ghosts of long-dead people, while others were the lingering essence of the recently departed, just waiting to enter the next world.

These ghosts and visions of the others were so common in my life that I nearly stopped noticing them. They never tried to hurt me or scare me, and in hindsight I've often wondered if they lived in my house to protect me and comfort me. My father was a more frightening entity than any shadowy human or phantom voice.

CHAPTER 3

Two women, two murders and a bird

My father sold burial insurance so that funeral expenses would not add to the burden of grief already being shouldered by those who had lost a loved one. He used to tell people that everybody's going to die so better to get a discount now than trying to get one after you're dead.

He kept his client list in black book of insurance policies, and he knew all of them personally. Every few months, when I was a little girl too young for school, I'd ride with him to collect his premiums, and in doing so I met many interesting people, and learned a great deal about my father along the way.

As a little girl, I could usually avoid my father's beatings by keeping quiet about the ghosts I saw and the others I heard. I learned absolute obedience in those years, because with obedience came survival.

My father and I would ride to the small towns of Antioch, Red Springs, Lumber Bridge, Aberdeen and Pine Hurst, Pine Bluff, Whispering Pines, Lumberton, Fayetteville, Saint Paul's and Dundarrach that were spread throughout the sprawling state of North Carolina.

I had probably seen half the state by the time I was 4 years old, and the undertaker had shown it to me. I knew everybody on our route and they knew me. People always waved as we drove down those country roads. It didn't matter if we knew them or not as it was just part of the southern tradition to wave. People were considered rude if they failed to wave, nod or otherwise acknowledge a complete stranger.

One of my favorite stops was at old Zelma Bullard's. She was an Indian woman with long black hair and a limp. Rumor had it that her leg came off at night and it was made of wood. She reminded me of a pirate. She and her husband owned a little store on the way to the tiny town of Antioch.

Zelma and her husband sold barbecued pork chop sandwiches. Customers would get their own pork chop from a machine that spun around, and then help themselves to a loaf of white bread that was under the machine. The store also had big sour gumballs in a large jar on the top shelf. It wasn't much of a store but was the only one for probably 20 miles.

Zelma also sold boiled peanuts, and she always gave me some in a tiny brown paper bag. I loved to remove them from their shells and drop them in my Pepsi Cola.

Old Zelma had a unique bird in her store. His name was Bill and he could talk like no other bird. Bill was the color blue like the pictures of the ocean in magazines. His wings were made of gold and he had a huge beak compared to most birds. Little did I know, Bill would soon be coming for a stay at our morgue.

Zelma was married to Robert, and the two of them

had a herd of children for me to play with while my daddy collected money for burial insurance. Children seldom came to my house to play, so I always looked forward to these trips with the undertaker. I also looked forward to seeing the people along the route, as they were some of the nicest individuals I have ever met. They were hard working, good Southern folks just trying to make a living.

Winnie Cameron's place was another favorite stop. She lived in an old house set back from the main road. Her house was across from a peach orchard on the road towards Aberdeen, and she made the best sweet pickles in the county.

Ms. Winnie would always reach under her kitchen sink to give me a jar to take home. A different jar under the sink held money, which she gave to my father for her insurance policy. She had several jars down there.

Ms. Winnie's husband had supposedly disappeared for no reason one day back in 1944. The townspeople said he went to the store and never came back. Winnie told investigators the same thing in 1944 when they started asking about her husband's whereabouts. And they believed her.

Thirty-four years would pass before Edward Cameron was located. His body, or what was left of it, was discovered in an old outhouse on Ms. Winnie's property. He had been chopped up with a hatchet.

Police had reopened the case of Edward and Winnie

Cameron in 1978 after one of their children told FBI officials that she had information relevant to her father's murder.

Annie Blue Cameron Perry was, in 1978, living in Florida and teaching at a community college. She told investigators that she had recently undergone psychotherapy in which therapists helped her probe childhood memories that Annie Perry didn't know existed.

Perry said the therapy had helped her recall Easter Sunday in 1944, when, at the age of 10, Annie stood in the family's kitchen and watched her mother dismember her father's corpse before throwing his remains in the pit of the family's privy, according to an article in the *Virginian-Pilot*.

The FBI persuaded Hoke County Sheriff Dave Barrington to reopen the case, and on Dec. 12, 1978, a backhoe uncovered the bones of a man fitting the size and age of the long-dead Edward Cameron. No positive ID could be made because no skull was found with the remains, the newspaper article states.

Barrington did not immediately arrest the aging Ms. Winnie Cameron, and one night was all she needed to write a letter confessing to the 34-year-old murder and then shoot herself in the head. Sheriff Barrington then destroyed Ms. Winnie's confession for reasons he never explained.

The Cameron case made national headlines in 1978, and not just because of its Southern Gothic details. The case marked the first time that repressed memories recovered during therapy were used to help solve a crime, according to the *Virginian-Pilot* article.

I was 15 when Ms. Winnie confessed to the murder and then killed herself, and the whole town was talking about the murder, the suicide and the bizarre sequence of events. But I always remembered her as the friendly, country woman who kept the county's best sweet pickles in a jar under her kitchen sink.

And as far as I know, Ms. Winnie Cameron never met Zelma Bullard, but they shared a common bond: both women murdered their husbands.

I was one of the first to know about Zelma's crime because I was trained at a young age to answer the telephone properly. Most people say "Hello?" but the greeting at my house was different. I didn't realize how different it was until kindergarten, when a bunch of us would pretend play with a plastic telephone.

I remember playing with another little girl in class, pretending to call her house. When I called, she said, "Hello?" When it was my turn to answer the phone, I said, "Lentz Mortuary," just as daddy had taught me.

The kids all laughed at me, and although I didn't know what I was saying, I knew it wasn't right. For the first time in my life, I was embarrassed; as if I had walked into a boy's bathroom with everyone watching. I was mortified, and I knew at that moment that I did not fit in.

Even though my telephone greeting was comical to the other children, it served me well at home, and one day shortly after the ridicule at school, I answered the phone at home with my usual, "Lentz Mortuary."

Zelma was on the other end, and she was crying. Apparently mistaking my voice for that of my mother, Zelma told me she had shot her husband, Robert.

Whenever someone died, things changed in my house, and I knew the undertaker would soon be helping get Robert ready to meet his Maker.

But this funeral was different than most. Zelma's children would not speak to her because she had blown their sleeping father away with a shotgun. She shot him dead center in the head – twice.

The family was insisting on an open casket in the middle of a hot summer. Their request – and the summer heat – posed a problem for the undertaker. Air conditioning was not common in the 60s, and the condition of Robert's forehead – or lack thereof – meant my father would need a great deal of makeup that could melt off the body and stain the casket lining.

The undertaker did the work of a Hollywood makeup artist on Robert. He managed to pull off an open casket viewing, and bury Robert Bullard in a black suit. My father placed my momma's beige table cloth over the white casket lining to prevent stains. Everybody thought Robert had a customized casket. They were impressed. Daddy could have charged the family extra for his work but I don't think he did.

People claimed Robert was sleeping with Zelma's sister and every other skirt in town. Most churchgoing people thought Robert deserved to die and felt bad for Zelma. My father may have been one of them.

He promised Zelma he would keep Bill, the blue bird, until Zelma went to court. No one could predict the outcome, but her children and family would have nothing to do with Zelma or her blue macaw.

My family didn't know anything about birds, but the undertaker put Bill in the basement because he whistled loudly and cursed frequently.

Bill was in the basement during Robert's viewing. Zelma was also there wearing handcuffs and escorted by the sheriff. As she entered the dining room where everyone was seated, Zelma apologized for what she had done, her voice carrying through her small nose.

The bird must have recognized her voice and began to talk, although the mourners could not see where the voice was coming from.

"Sorry bastard should have died a long time ago," echoed through the funeral home just as the minister was leading the family in prayer.

I think some astonished mourners thought God was talking, but the undertaker wore a look of instant fury. I expected him to embalm the bird and bury him with Robert after the outburst. Instead, he decided immediately that Bill would be placed outside for all future funerals.

Despite the bird's outburst, the undertaker kept his promise to Zelma and Bill lived with us for the eight years of Zelma's incarceration. She came to get the bird upon her release from prison, and I never saw her again.

While Robert's murder was an unusual exception, other deaths were part of the daily, household routine at Lentz Mortuary.

First the phone would ring. Then the undertaker would go somewhere to retrieve the corpse and bring it home in the back of the hearse. From there, he and my mother would move a sheet-draped stretcher into the basement.

I always knew then that the smell of death was imminent. It wafted through the entire house as that crystal doorknob turned and echoed – the sound of my father entering the embalming room; the sound of my childhood.

A few days after the undertaker performed his mysterious work in the basement, the casket would be displayed in the parlor for the viewing and funeral services.

As you walked in the front entrance of our house, you could see the door leading into the basement. The pedestal for the memorial book was to the right of the door. A long room known as the parlor stretched to the right of the book stand. It featured two windows covered by dark gray drapes that were always closed.

The casket was always in the same place in this parlor – in front of the window with a small floor lamp creating a slight ambiance. This was the only light in the room. The walls were light gray and the floor was covered with a dull gray carpet. A hundred or so wooden folding chairs would be lined up for the mourners. I saw thousands of mourners during my childhood, and I learned what grief looked like at a very young age. Many tears were shed in our dining room as more than 1,300 people died while I lived at Lentz Mortuary.

My childhood on West Prospect Avenue may not be considered normal by today's standards, but what exactly is normal, and does anyone truly fit anyone else's definition? Our society's perception of normal is constantly changing, but I always knew that I was different.

CHAPTER 4
Buried Memories

Graveyards are not usually familiar places for small children. Rather, they are the stuff of sleepover ghost stories, and jokes about people dying to get in. But throughout my childhood, I was routinely exposed to cemeteries, graves and burials.

On bright spring days, a well-groomed graveyard exudes serene and tranquil beauty. Magnolia trees, with their fragrant, white flowers, outline the Raeford cemetery, which is located across from a turkey processing plant. The trees and flowers were intended to take people's minds off the dead bodies that lay just 6 feet below.

North Carolina law requires that all dead bodies be placed at least 6 feet under the earth's surface. Digging a hole that deep is a tough job, made even more difficult when the ground is frozen during the winter months. A grave digger had to pry through the earth's frozen layers, and thick, black gloves became the digger's best friend.

When someone died, the cemetery in which the body was to be buried was the first order of business because digging had to be arranged immediately. Winter and holidays can prolong the excavation process, as grave diggers were self-employed men with families, and many of them refused to work on holidays. Grave diggers weren't listed in the yellow pages, and some people back then did not have a phone in their home. Many diggers had other jobs, and were not always available on a moment's notice. At times, I remember my father leaving the house with a shovel and digging a burial plot himself.

Despite the undertaker's faults, he was a fair man who understood people's various financial situations. I recall many occasions in which the only fee he collected was the money collected in an old black hat that was passed during the funeral.

Death always comes as a shock, and most people have given no thought to funeral plans or the cost of them. Many undertakers exploit people's despair and take advantage of the grieving relatives. I can say with all honesty that my daddy was not in that category.

One particular burial stands out in my mind both for its oddity, and the fact that a great deal of thought obviously had gone into its planning.

In an effort to avoid embarrassing this particular woman's family, I will call this charitable woman Ms. Vera. Her funeral was one I will never forget – and it's the one that nearly killed my father.

Ms. Vera was a kind woman, with a heart as big as her massive frame. She was, quite possibly, the only person in Raeford who had ever adopted a child.

Most folks weren't even aware of it. I found out by overhearing a conversation about Ms. Vera's family burial insurance policy. My father swore me to secrecy and this is the first I have mentioned it.

After struggling with a thyroid problem her whole life and then being constantly sick toward the end of her life, Ms. Vera ultimately died in her sleep.

Her death – and her size – presented a dilemma for the undertaker. Ms. Vera was an obese woman and would not fit into a standard casket. Rather, the undertaker had to bury her in a piano case.

Unlike most folks, Ms. Vera had discussed her plans with the undertaker and was aware of the predicament that her death would present. In addition to the unusual casket, Ms. Vera's burial was remarkable in that she was buried in her own backyard rather than in the town cemetery.

The woman must have known that her days were limited because she had a wire fence built to mark her grave.

Unlike the rest of the town's dead people, Ms. Vera didn't arrive at our basement in the undertaker's hearse, but in the back of his old Ford pickup truck. And she wasn't on a stretcher. My mother had sewn four sheets together to accommodate the massive form, and my father recruited a small army of volunteers to hoist her out of the truck. The old basement door had to be removed from its hinges, and a few concrete blocks had to be removed.

Once my father was finished with the preparations, Ms. Vera would exit the funeral home the same way she entered, and would not be laid out in the parlor.

I remember when the piano case was delivered to our house. The undertaker again called in the troops to lay Ms. Vera inside and transport the giant crate to her backyard.

But the day before Ms. Vera was to be buried; my father and I went to her house to check the progress of her grave. It was a frigid winter that year and the excavation had been taking longer than usual.

It was pouring when we arrived, and we could just make out two tents that covered Ms. Vera's grave. One of the tent stakes had come out of the ground. My father got out of the truck to investigate and told me to stay where I was.

But several hours then passed and I became worried. The rain continued relentlessly and the mountain of dirt from Ms. Vera's grave looked to be getting smaller.

I finally got out of the car to find my father and headed toward the dirt pile. When I reached the tent covering the grave, and the remaining dirt next to it, I found my father inside the over-sized grave. He had fallen in, and the dirt that had been piled on the side of the hole was washing in on him. The undertaker was being buried alive right before my very eyes. I quickly tied one of the ropes from the tent to the car door so my father could pull himself out of the hole.

He was covered in mud from head to toe, and for the first time in my life, my father was speechless.

The rain finally let up as we left Ms. Vera's, and my father was grateful to be alive. On the way home, we stopped by the Raeford cemetery, where a rooster had lived for as long as I could remember.

I had always wanted to bring the funny bird home with us, and on this day my father put the bird in the back of the hearse and thanked me for saving his life. The undertaker took a liking to that old rooster, which only made noise in the early morning. We named the rooster Mr. Vera, and though he turned out to be mean as hell, he was also the best playmate I ever had.

Ms. Vera's burial went as planned, and I ended up with a pet rooster. The undertaker used to make jokes about making bird nest soup out of Mr. Vera, but I always thought the jokes people made about the undertaker were funnier.

My father didn't always agree, and I remember the time Otis Crowder from next door gave me a quarter to answer our telephone by saying, "Lentz Mortuary – you stab 'em, we slab 'em."

When I finally worked up the courage to try this new

greeting, it wasn't Otis calling, but the undertaker himself and he was mad as hell. The undertaker and Otis had a long talk that day, and I'm sure I got beaten, but the joke became one of my fondest memories.

CHAPTER 5
Runaway Hearse

Life in a funeral home does produce an impressive collection of bizarre tales that would have been more fun to recount if our home had been a happier one. My parents could have retired to Florida and been popular with the shuffleboard crowd with their tales of funeral mishaps. The elderly crowd is quick to laugh about death, and there's a certain amount of gallows humor in retirement communities.

That crowd would have enjoyed the story of Margaret Sanders, even more so because they didn't know Margaret, and they didn't have to listen to how livid my father was the whole day after her casket slid out the back of the hearse and interrupted a nearby cemetery service.

Death is never a laughing matter, and my father treated his clients with the utmost care and respect. I recount this story, not to make fun of anyone, but to share just one of the odd memories produced by my childhood.

Besides, when you write a book about growing up in a funeral home, you have to include the obligatory chapter on strange events, dead bodies and humorous happenings.

The story of Margaret Sanders was not at all amusing when it happened, around 1969. I was 6 years old, and Margaret's husband, Marvin, was my godfather. He was a friend of my father's, and a regular customer at his antique shop.

I still have the Charlie MacArthur puppet Marvin gave me for my fifth birthday. Marvin and Margaret lived in a big, white farmhouse with Marvin's brother, John, who never spoke. People all said that a cat had gotten his tongue, but I never understood what they meant.

John was the tall brother, and just grunted on occasion. Marvin was short and friendly, and he reminded me of a skinny Santa Claus. But on the day of Margaret's burial, no one was smiling.

My father handled Margaret's funeral and arrangements, but she was not to be buried in Raeford Cemetery. She was to be buried near Rockingham, I believe, and I remember riding with my father in the hearse to the distant cemetery around Thanksgiving.

When we arrived, my father drove to the top of the hill that the cemetery was carved into. We saw John and Marvin standing with a few others who were there to help move the casket.

My father told me to wait in the hearse, and he left it running with the heat on while he exited the vehicle and approached the other men.

But gravity began to tug at the hearse, which had no emergency brake. It started rolling backward down the cemetery hill with Margaret and me still inside. My father and the other men chased the accelerating car down the hill, but it just kept picking up speed.

I had seen my father press the pedal on the left side under the steering wheel to slow us down on our many trips around the state. So I crawled under the wheel and pushed on the brake with both hands.

It worked, and the car stopped immediately. Unfortunately, Margaret kept going. Her casket slid out the back of the hearse, down the steep hill until it came to rest against a tree. The lid opened, revealing the disheveled body of Margaret, and thoroughly interrupting the graveside service taking place just a few yards away.

My father spent the rest of the day trying to reassure Marvin and making things right. We dropped Margaret off at a nearby funeral home to fix her up and complete the required tasks.

My father swore the whole way home. It was late when we got home to Raeford, and I later realized that was the last time I would ever see Marvin, but I still have the puppet he gave me.

That old black hearse was a permanent fixture in our driveway and in my childhood. My father drove the hearse or his old Ford pick-up truck. My mother didn't drive at all, and was completely dependent on my father for nearly everything. I realized later that this gave my father complete control over my mother. It kept her from leaving him, because even if she had the nerve to escape, she did not have the means.

I practiced driving in our circular driveway, and probably put 1,000 miles on the hearse just going in circles, and dreaming of the day I would drive out of Raeford forever.

I also used the roof of the hearse as a sundeck during the summer. I would flatten a large box and cover it with tin foil to capture the sun's rays. I spread the flattened box on the roof of the hearse, and climbed on top of it in my bathing suit, folding up the side flaps. In this way, I was shielded from the view of anyone walking down the street, and ensured that the sun's most harmful rays were being beamed directly onto my adolescent skin.

But it was the 70s. Everyone wanted a tan, and skin cancer was the least of our worries in that decade.

CHAPTER 6
Holidays at Lentz Mortuary

I tracked the seasonal approach of Christmas every year like a South Florida weatherman tracks a hurricane. It was a wonderful time of year, and the joyous holiday made up for the bleak weather that accompanied it.

Winter ripped the colorful leaves from barren and lifeless trees. An endless gray sky would fill with black crows, and eventually snow would fall.

The cold outside always managed to penetrate our home. Most houses had a pot belly stove, a fireplace or furnace. My house had all three, but the chill always remained. As the cold moved in, the furnace pilot would have to be lit. The old floor furnace produced an awful musty smell and groaned like a sick person.

Heat is supposed to give the feeling of warmth and comfort, but the heat from the old furnace only produced dampness. You could stand on it for hours and still shake and shiver. I remember blowing onto the window inside my house and being able to write my name on the freezing glass. One time my finger felt like it had been stung by a bee in the midst of winter, but it was actually frost bite.

The anticipation of Christmas made the winter bearable, and each year I wished on a red cardinal that no one would die at Christmas.

The red cardinal is the state bird of North Carolina and

was my favorite. I rested all my hopes for the Christmas season on that bird and its folklore. My mother taught me the old saying, "See a red bird, touch blue and make a wish and it will come true."

A death at Christmas meant that my beloved Christmas tree, with its warmth and light, had to come down. There was never anything fancy on our tree but it had a way of bringing those deathly rooms to life. I have seen many Christmas trees in my time but never one with the power to make me feel warm and comfortable the way those funeral home trees did.

My father and I would go out to old Highway 211 every year and find the perfect Douglas fir. We would either chop our own or purchase one from the tent, and then the tree had to sit for 24 hours before it could be decorated.

I have some good memories of tree-shopping with my father, and usually if I kept very quiet, I could prevent a tantrum from him that was often accompanied by a beating.

Our Christmas lights were the typical oval, multi-colored bulbs on endless strands of wire. Many of our ornaments were antiques, along with a variety of hand-blown glass birds that were placed strategically on the tree. A white dove was always close to the top.

Our Christmas tree was installed every year in the parlor

– where the caskets were displayed. And every year it was removed if there was to be a viewing in the parlor. The undertaker said it was not appropriate for grieving people to be reminded of the season. He told me it was selfish for me not to understand. Our beautiful tree had to be taken down many times at Christmas, and it was never put back up after a funeral.

I cried myself to sleep on many a Christmas Eve, wondering if Santa would be able to find a house so filled with death and darkness. Despite my concerns, I always left cookies and milk for him in the parlor whether it was occupied by a beautiful Christmas tree or a dead body.

While most folks in Raeford were singing carols and sharing a decadent Christmas Eve meal, my family often was hearing mournful hymns and eating cereal. My mother was not allowed to cook if someone was laid to rest in the parlor. My father said the smell of the food would be a distraction to mourners, so I ate many bowls of Cap'n Crunch and Boo Berry cereal instead of turkey, goose or other traditional holiday feasts. When people later asked how my Christmas was, my father would tell them I had had a wonderful holiday. He often answered questions for me, apparently worried that I would tell the truth. No one knew that a 5-year-old girl had to take her Christmas tree down to make room for a dead body. My father wouldn't tell anyone what really happened at our house.

He always told me that having a mother and father was a Christmas gift in itself, and that I should be grateful for what I had. And although the statement puzzled my 5-year-old mind, I eventually came to know how right he was. But I also understand now that my father may have been subconsciously reminding me and himself that his life would have turned out differently had he left that pregnant, country girl named LaRue alone.

In the years that saw no deaths at Christmas, I had a wonderful time opening presents and then spending the day at my Great Aunt Marguerite's house. My family always spent Christmas Day, or at least an hour of it, together.

We walked the three blocks to my Aunt Marguerite's wonderful home, where a brightly colored package and striped candy cane was waiting for me under the tree. And what a majestic tree it was – the exact one that Santa himself would proudly have displayed at the North Pole.

Aunt Marguerite opened her house and her heart to distant and immediate family every year, and the time we spent at her house as a family almost made up for the family vacations we never took. Of course, we were all together at my aunt's house for only an hour or so because someone always had to be home to answer the call of death. My mother or father usually left after an hour, but I could stay longer in my great aunt's beautiful home. She had a way of making Christmas and every day special for everyone around her.

The present from Aunt Marguerite was in addition to the ones I would open at home, many of which came from my father's antique shop. He would bring presents home to me from people who dropped them off at his shop. I never liked going into the dusty shop. Everything was old and decaying and required tremendous care. But I happily tore into any gift that he brought home from the musty shop. And in all my childhood, I only broke one vase.

One Christmas Eve the undertaker and I had been at the antique shop, on our way home stopped at a house on the outskirts of town.

The family we visited had no Christmas tree or presents in their house. I thought perhaps their Christmas had been canceled like so many of mine, and I looked furtively for the casket I assumed must be in one of the rooms. But no, I was the only child who lived in a funeral home. This family simply couldn't afford the warm festivities of the holiday.

Clyde, the father, was a mechanic with an old, rundown gas station. Imogene was his heavyset and sickly wife who didn't work. I used to play with their children, Theresa and Harvey, when my father collected their burial insurance payments. They didn't have much, but I enjoyed our time at their house on the edge of town.

After leaving their house that Christmas Eve and returning home, my father took down our tree, along with some ornaments and lights. He then suggested that I give Theresa a few of the gifts that were wrapped underneath it and awaiting my eager hands the next morning.

The idea first made me weep with the thought of what I was losing. But the undertaker had a way of looking into my eyes so I could see and feel his instant disapproval without him saying a word.

I did as my father asked and we returned to the house on the outskirts of town. He placed our tree and my presents on the front porch before driving off without a word to the family.

In fact, he didn't say a word to anyone except my mother, who deserved to know what had happened to our tree.

The undertaker told me not to tell anyone what we did, and explained the concepts of dignity and pride to a little girl. He said you had to have money to live, but that money does not determine who you are or what you're really worth in this world. My father said no one had ever asked to be buried with their money, and he would know, because he spent his life honoring people's last wishes.

He also said that a good deed is worth nothing at all if you have to tell someone else that you did it. The undertaker always said that every man was born with pride and every man should leave this earth with some of it intact.

My father was by no means a rich man, and he eventually accumulated a healthy share of debt. But in 1969 he taught me the true meaning of Christmas, and I would always remember the year I learned that Christmas is about helping others and being willing to share whatever you have with someone less fortunate.

And while Christmas seemed to bring out the best in my father, Halloween was a different event entirely. Despite the typical neighborhood bravado that included ghostly tales and dares to sneak into the basement, very few trick-or-treaters were actually brave enough to ring our doorbell. And of course, if someone died on Halloween, everything changed.

Death would cancel my costumed trick-or-treating adventure and I would be relegated to the house, as my father said it would be impolite for me to be coming and going in costume during a service. Instead I was expected to lend my youthful optimism to mourners, who seemed to view children as a sign of life in times of death. Mourners always wanted to know where Ina was.

I do remember a few Halloweens when I placed fake dead people on the porch. I stuffed old clothes with newspapers and made their head out of a paper sack with a mask and wig on top, but I stopped this practice when the noises I always heard coming from the basement started intensifying. We'll get to that later.

Birthdays were a happier occasion, and always included a homemade cake with ice cream on top and a few guests. Most of our guests were adults, but sometime I could invite a few friends over. They would sing "Happy Birthday" during an outdoor party despite the grave markers in our backyard and a circular driveway that was lined with chunks of tombstone. I used to walk on them, pretending they were a bridge over a winding path.

An old picnic table sat on the side of our house near the dogwood that was the first tree I learned to climb. It was always in bloom for my April birthday, and the tree produced my mother's favorite white, cross-shaped flowers.

There was a dark brown spot on the edge of each petal, which my grandmother always said was put there by God to remind people of the Crucifixion. She said the spot in the middle represented the stain on the cross.

Easter was a day for church, and you've already heard that my parents' anniversary was no cause for celebration. They never went anywhere without me except the basement morgue, there were no family vacations, and we rarely even went to church as a family because someone had to answer the phone.

But there was one occasion in our home that was unaffected by death. The tooth fairy always stopped at the funeral home – always. Even during a death, I could always count on it. No spook or ghost could keep it away. Unfortunately, the tooth fairy could not keep the ghosts of the house away from me.

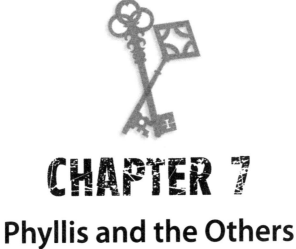

CHAPTER 7
Phyllis and the Others

I was four years old in 1967, and had been seeing ghosts and other people, caught between this world and the next, for much of my remembered childhood. Some were ghosts that had decided to live among us, while I came to know the others as spirits who had not yet crossed over. They resembled the images of people, but were not quite human – like shadows that someone's figure casts on a bare wall, but more personal.

I don't know why these spirits chose to hang around the site of their funeral, but my parents routinely dismissed my sightings, and attributed the noises I would frequently hear to a wild imagination. My father decided that I had an imaginary friend, while my mother admonished me for fibbing.

Their reaction confused my 4-year-mind, which had learned not to say things that were untrue. But I also learned that any mention of what I saw resulted in a severe beating, which became more frequent as I got older, more vocal and more curious.

One evening in 1967, someone else finally saw Phyllis – or the ghost of her.

Phyllis was an older African-American woman who had taken care of me for the first three years of my life. My mother had kept her job at the phone company until Phyllis died. She had to walk several blocks each morning to the bus stop, and then ride into Fayetteville for work. She then walked home from the bus stop every night, winter or spring, rain or snow. My father certainly was not going to drive her to and from work, but throughout my childhood, I never remember him once giving my mother a ride to or from the bus stop.

My mother stopped working to take care of me after Phyllis died. My father handled her funeral arrangements and burial.

After her death, I saw Phyllis daily, always in the parlor where the caskets were placed during services. She would appear, hovering two feet off the floor, every evening after sunset. But every time I mentioned her appearance to my father, he denied seeing anything, and told me to stop talking nonsense.

I was never frightened by her appearance, and in fact was comforted by her familiar presence. She knew the workings of our family, and I sort of figured she was there to continue keeping an eye on me.

One winter evening, I was playing with my friend, Lisa Crowder, who was a few years older and lived next door. Her brother, Otis, and one of her cousins occasionally helped my father with funerals, and Mrs. Crowder made the town's best biscuits and gravy, so we usually played at her house. It was rare for me to have friends over at our house. My father was not necessarily welcoming, and no one wanted to spend time in a house that also contained dead bodies.

I never told Lisa about Phyllis's regular visits. She was a skittish child who scared easily and would have refused to enter our home. She was afraid to walk home past a scary tree, and would call her mother before leaving our house so her mother could watch for her from their front door.

But the evening we both saw Phyllis, Lisa and I were playing a game in front of our living room fireplace. The details that lodge in one's memory during these memorable events are intriguing in their specificity.

I distinctly recall our game of "Barrel of Monkeys," which involved connecting a chain of plastic monkeys. I also remember glancing at the clock, because although I could not yet tell time, I knew that Phyllis often appeared when the big hand was on the 12 and the small hand near the 7.

From our position in the living room, we could see directly into the parlor where funerals took place. When Phyllis appeared in her usual location, I quietly touched Lisa and pointed to the parlor.

Lisa dropped her monkeys and started screaming, immediately capturing my mother's attention. She came running and told me to stop telling tales that scared people.

Lisa never again visited our house after dark, and would not speak of what she had seen for 40 years. I contacted Lisa while writing this chapter, and though she could not remember the specific details, she has never forgotten Phyllis.

But Phyllis apparently forgot about us, because I didn't see her as regularly after that evening. I always assumed Lisa's screaming had, in fact, scared away a ghost.

It feels as if I saw more ghosts when I was young than I did as a teen-ager, although perhaps by then I had simply become so accustomed to them that I failed to notice their presence. As crazy as it seems, that was my laid-back attitude about the "others" who lived in our house. I saw those ghostly images, heard voices, moans and other sounds. Doors would open and close by themselves and lights would go on and off. These occurrences became a way of life – my way of life, but I was never allowed to discuss them with anyone. People didn't speak of ghosts or hauntings or bizarre intuitions back then, especially not in a funeral home, where such talk was crippling for business.

But time would tell, as it always does. The truth took decades to be revealed, and in a way, the story of that house continues to this day.

Jim Lentz, with his mother, Ina Elizabeth Lentz Paulsen, in 1957, standing in the parlor of Lentz Mortuary.

Author's grandmother and namesake, Ina Elizabeth Lentz Paulsen, 1964

Jim, LaRue and Ina Lentz in the parlor of Lentz Mortuary, circa 1965

The author, Ina Lentz Griesbeck, after graduating from high school in 1981.

Ina and her mother at Sun Bridge Rest Home, 1998

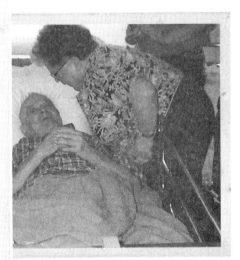

The author and her father in 1986 in Florida

LaRue Brennan Lentz forgiving Jim Lentz, in Raeford Manor Rest Home two weeks before Jim Lentz's death, 2000

June 1979- Raeford *News-Journal*

Baby Died In '30; Burial Now In Sight

The embalmed body of an infant had lain in a box in a local funeral home since its death 35 to 40 tears ago till Monday, Raeford Police Chief Leonard Wiggins reported Monday night.

He said an investigation showed nothing illegal involved.

The body would have been buried years ago, he said, but for the inability of the funeral home director, James Lentz, to get information necessary for him to obtain burial permit.

Several people have known about the body being in the funeral home, but no attempt was ever made to remove it, though it was not in the knowledge of the general public according to the chief investigation shows.

Apparently, no police investigation had been made before Sunday night because no complaint had been made to the police department.

This started the movement to an investigation of what to do about the report which was received by department at 11:22PM according to Wiggins.

He said Cindy and Gail Baker, Raeford sisters, told police they had been told by Ina Lentz, 16 that the body of a baby was in the basement of the funeral home, at 411 W. Prospect Ave.

Policemen Rodney Collins and Jim Madden, whom the girls talked to, talked with Mrs. James Lentz, Ina's mother, shortly afterward.

Mrs. Lentz gave the officers permission to check and showed them where the body was, Wiggins said. He said the policeman found in the embalmment room area the petrified body of the infant.

Dr. Robert Townsend, a Hoke county medical examiner called to the mortuary by the police, ordered the body sent to the state chief medical examiners' office in Chapel Hill.

Wiggins said Dr. Butts of the chief examiners' staff telephoned him from Chapel Hill Monday afternoon that the body was that of a "full-term (nine months)" infant and death had resulted from natural causes. Dr. Butts told the officer no evidence of fowl play had been found.

The doctor said the condition of the body made it impossible for the examiner to determine the sex or race of the child.

He said he couldn't be exact but the child had been dead 35 to 40 years.

The examination also showed an autopsy had been performed on the body at the time of death.

Lentz told Wiggins he bought the McDiarmid Funeral Home (then near Niven's Appliance & Furniture Co. at 116 N. Main St.) in 1947 and moved it to it's present location in 1948.

Lentz told the officer he was unaware the body existed till several months later at the new location when he discovered it in a box while he was moving boxes.

He said a McDiarmid employee he talked to told him he was told about the case 10 years before, that the body had been embalmed but that the identity of the child was unknown.

Lentz said that in 1952 he tried to get a Hoke County Health Department permit to bury the body at his own expense but was refused because he couldn't answer questions on the permit.

Wiggins said Lentz was "very delighted proper authorities" had the body because he had not wanted to keep it.

"I expect the chief medical examiner's office will take steps to have the proper thing done." Wiggins said.

There is no way we can go further," he added. "To my knowledge, everyone involved (in the baby's background) is deceased."

One rumor is he said, the baby was stillborn, and the mother's then dead boday was taken to the McDiarmid Funeral Home, but they did not bury the baby with her.

"News-Journal" article about the decomposing infant found in the author's basement.

The skeleton keys and doorknob that provided access to the foreboding basement of Lentz Mortuary

The undertaker, James C. Lentz, in front of Lentz Mortuary

The author, Ina, with parents, LaRue and Jim Lentz, circa 1973

LaRue Brennan Lentz, 1971

"News-Journal" article about the house at 411 West Prospect Avenue

Former funeral home hau[nted]

"When I moved in there, I don't know if it is my imagination or what, but I did see a gentleman in there...I went to bed and saw him standing in the doorway. It scared me to death." – Nettie Adams

By Jason Beck
Staff Writer

Ina Lentz Griesbeck and Nettie Adams have never met, however, they do share a common bond. Both have lived in the two-story house at 411 West Prospect Street in Raeford.

Though their stays in the house are separated by more than 30 years, both are convinced the house is haunted.

Sure the broken windows, looming frame and creepy basement give off the haunted vibe, but it is the 1,300 or so dead bodies that once
(See HAUNTED, page 4A)

Strange things happen in t[he]

Zelma Bullard's macaw, Bill, who lived for eight years at Lentz Mortuary

Ms. Winnie's House where I went as a little girl with my father.

June 2009 - Raeford *News-Journal*

Haunted

continued from 1A)

...d in the home that attract the ...osts, Griesbeck says.

Griesbeck's father, James Lentz, ...vned the home and operated ...entz's Funeral Home at the lo-...tion for years. Griesbeck, who ...w lives in Hollywood, Florida, is ...riting a book about her childhood ...rowing up in a funeral home.

If These Walls Could Speak ...ends much time talking about ...e ghostly happenings inside the ...ouse.

"My bedroom was downstairs, ...vo doors away from the bodies," ...riesbeck said. "When you walked ...to the house there was the front ...oor, then there was a dining room ...nd that's where the casket would ...o."

Of course the bodies were em-...almed in the basement. Griesbeck ...aid none of her friends would ...ream of even going down there.

She said there were many spiri-...ual happenings in the dwelling as ...he was growing up.

"I wouldn't be a very spiritual ...erson if I didn't there was another ...imension out there," she said. "...Vhen I was at the fireplace, play-...ng , looking across to the dining ...oom, that's where I saw the people ...ross over. I remember it like it was ...esterday.

"A couple of times bodies stood ...up on the embalming table," she ...said. I know when, I liked there me ...nd my mother heard noises all the ...ime. No one is going to live in that ...house for a long period of time."

It would be easy to dismiss Griesbeck's stories as crazy, lies or childhood imagination. However, Adams' time in the house comes into play.

Adams, who works at the Hoke County Library, is the home's current resident. She knew of the home's history before she moved in and isn't fazed by the ghosts at all— even after seeing one.

When I moved in there, I don't know if it is my imagination or what, but I did see a gentleman in there," Adams said. " I went to bed and saw him standing in the doorway. It scared me to death."

Since then, Adams said, there have been plenty of other strange happenings around the house.

"Stuff disappears and then reappears in places you know that you looked," she said."one time I lost my keys on Friday and didn't find the until Monday. They were on the headboard of the bed and I know I looked there.

"I've not had any bad experiences," she said. "I hear noises but you hear noises in all old houses."

Adams has lived in the house for two years, and says there's no sign it was ever a funeral home, except for the drain the in the basement that would pump out the embalming fluid or blood or whatever stained the floors.

She said she's heard rumors the funeral home shut down because the owner 'played house with the bodies.' However, Griesbeck said a strange event in 1979 could have been her father's funeral home's downfall.

As a sophomore at Hoke High, Ina told her fiends about a dead baby being stored in the basement of the house. Her friends reported the nuews to their families who then called the police.

When approached, Mr. Lentz showed the body to the police officers. He said he found the body in the basement after buying the funeral home from a previous owner. Since he couldn't identify the body, he was unable to acquire a proper permit to bury it.

According to *News-Journal* articles written at the time, the body was more than 30 years old and was traced to a mother who died during childbirth. Somehow the baby's body was overlooked.

Griesbeck said the publicity garnered by the dead infant and stiff competition from nearby Crumpler's funeral home dealt a blow to the Lentz operation. She said by the time she left the home after high school, her father's funeral business was basically over.

Griesbeck says there's more to her book than just ghost stories> Growing up in a funeral home is an unusual life. She learned to drive using the family hearse. Even holidays were different.

"I always prayed that no one would die at Christmas time, because we would have to take down the Christmas tree," she said. "That's where the casket would go."

The book is still in it's rough stages and may not be finished for another year, the writer said. She said the most important thing people need to remember is that the ghosts in the house don't want to do harm.

"One thing my father always said was it is the people who are living that hurt you." She said.

Adams is on of the few people to live at peace with the home's ghosts. She even hosted a Halloween haunted house there two years ago.

"In my long life I've learned the dead cannot hurt you, but if you are afraid you can hurt yourself," she said. "I figure if they didn't want me there they would have made me leave a long time ago."

THE FAYETTEVILLE OBSERVER | LOCAL & STATE

ASSISTED LIVING CENTER

Fire shuts Raeford Manor

By Nancy McCleary
Staff writer

RAEFORD — More than 50 residents of the Raeford Manor assisted living center were displaced after a fire Wednesday shut the facility down.

Although the fire was confined to one room, the center at 110 Campus Ave. sustained smoke and water damage throughout, said Raeford Fire Marshal Terry Tapp.

The residents have been moved to other centers in the area, he said.

The cause of the fire has not been determined, Tapp

 Sign up for @lerts
■ Get breaking news delivered to your e-mail. Sign up for @lerts at fayobserver.com.

said, but it is not believed to be suspicious.

The State Bureau of Investigation is assisting the Raeford Fire Department in trying to pinpoint what started the blaze, Tapp said.

The fire was reported about 2:30 p.m.

By the time the first firefighters arrived, center workers had started evacuating people who lived there, Tapp said.

They were taken to the fellowship hall at a church across the street from the facility, Tapp said.

The main hallway was filled with smoke when firefighters arrived, Tapp said.

"Shortly after we got there, the fire came out through a window," he said.

Firefighters spent the first five to 10 minutes looking for one resident who could not be found. The man was found unharmed in a bathroom, Tapp said.

Eight residents and about four workers were taken to area hospitals, including Cape Fear Valley Medical Center and FirstHealth Moore Regional Hospital, Tapp said. No one was seriously injured, Tapp said. Most were complaining of smoke inhalation.

The fire destroyed the room where it started and damaged neighboring rooms, Tapp said.

Raeford Manor will be closed until repairs are made and utilities can be restored, he said.

Staff writer Nancy McCleary can be reached at mcclearyn@fayobserver.com or 486-3568.

An article in The Fayetteville Observer recounted the fire at Raeford Manor, which started mysteriously the day of LaRue Lentz's private viewing.

Of Baby's Death

The baby whose embalmed body remained in a local Funeral home unclaimed for over 40 years was dead when it was delivered at birth and the child's mother died in labor with the child, the Raeford Police Department investigation has learned.

Police Chief Leonard Wiggins said last week the mother has been identified as Caroline Purcell and that she died January 10, 1936, at home.

He quoted James Archie Purcell, a brother of Ms. Purcell as saying he and other members of the family believed the baby and mother were buried in the same casket. This explained why the baby's body wasn't claimed.

James Lentz, owner and operator of Lentz Mortuary of Raeford, said last week he found the body in a box after he had moved the furnishings and equipment of McDiarmid Funeral Home from the Main Street quarters of McDiarming in 1948.

He bought the McDiarmid Funeral Home in 1947. Wiggins quoted Lentz as saying he wanted to bury the body at his own expense in 195_ but was unable to get a burial permit because he couldn't get the information required, including the identity of the parents.

Wiggins learned that an autopsy had been performed on the baby body shortly after death and examined by the state that death resulted from _____

The infant body found in the basement of Lentz Mortuary was eventually identified and properly laid to rest.

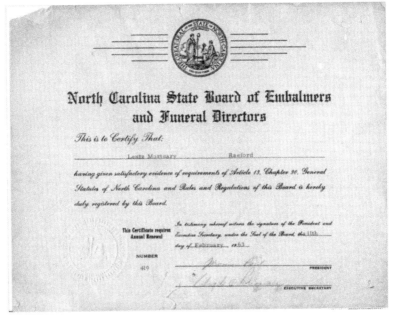

James C. Lentz's embalming license

Lentz Files Friday For Coroner's Slot

Veteran funeral director James C. Lentz filed Friday for the position of County Coroner, a job he had held for almost 10 years from 1948 to 1958.

The operator of Lentz Mortuary in Raeford, a concern he purchased from N. McL. Diarmid some 15 years ago, said:

"I had hoped that a qualified doctor would file for the position and I waited until the last-minute for this to happen. When it didn't, I felt that my 10 years experience in the Coroner's job entitled me to file."

Lentz thus opposes incumbent Frank Crumpler who is also a funeral director in Raeford.

The new entrant into the Coroner's race was born in Hoke County, the son of the late William F. Lentz and Mrs. Ina Lentz Paulsen of Raeford and Fort Lauderdale, Fla. He is the grandson of the late J. C. Thomas.

Lentz attended Raeford schools, Randolph-Macon Academy and Eckel College of Mortuary Science in Philadelphia. He is a licensed embalmer and funeral director, a Kiwanian, a Mason, a member of the Moose Lodge, past president of the Hoke-Raeford Jaycees and owner of the Raeford Memorial Company. His mortuary business is conducted with the help of five employees.

He succeeded the late W. L. Roper as Coroner in 1948, and was elected to two terms in that job in 1950 and 1954. He was defeated in a bid for re-election in 1958 by Dr. Bill Barry, whose resignation last year brought Crumpler in to fill out the unexpired term.

JIM LENTZ
...Runs for Coroner

Jim Lentz runs for county coroner

James C. Lentz

RAEFORD — James C. Lentz, 76, of 1100 Campus Ave. died Friday in FirstHealth Moore Regional Hospital in Pinehurst.

Mr. Lentz was the former owner of Lentz Mortuary in Raeford and Highland Antiques in Fayetteville.

The funeral will be conducted at 11 a.m. Wednesday in Raeford Presbyterian Church by Dr. John C. Ropp and the Rev. Kevin Campbell. Burial will be in Raeford City Cemetery. Arrangements are being handled by Highland Funeral Service & Crematory.

Mr. Lentz is survived by a daughter, Ina E. Griesbeck of Hollywood, Fla.; a sister, Edna Coughenhour of Fort Lauderdale, Fla.; and a grandson.

The family will receive friends Wednesday from 10 to 11 a.m. at the church.

Jim Lentz obituary, 2000

CHAPTER 8
Devastating Descent

As the years rolled by and the noises in my home or head grew louder, my prayers became more intense. I knelt faithfully on a brown velvet prayer stool as my mother had taught me, praying for normalcy in my life and in my house. I wanted to have close friends and normal holidays. I wanted people to believe my stories about ghosts and noises. I wanted to know that I wasn't crazy. I wanted to fit in, and most of all, I wanted to sleep without the nightmares that I brought on myself at age 10, when my curiosity got the best of me.

In my early childhood, I would see tiny specks of colors when I closed my eyes. My mother said they were a sign from the Sandman that it was time for bed. She must have been right, as I always fell fast asleep, often with the sound of funeral music filling the house. And it should come as no surprise that a child growing up in a funeral home with dead bodies in the basement would experience wild and bizarre dreams.

At age 10 I had to know the source of the sounds I heard and the ghosts I saw. I had to explore our basement. And as with most situations in my life, curiosity got the best of me and turned my dreams to nightmares.

I knew the undertaker kept the skeleton key to the basement in a purple goblet on the mantle over the fireplace.

I stood on one of the wooden mourner's chairs to reach the mantle, and reached carefully into the goblet. It contained several keys, but the skeleton key was – and still is – easily recognizable.

My mother had walked to Bob Harrell's grocery store three blocks away, so time was on my side. Mr. Harrell's conversation skills were legendary, and the walk itself was sure to include discussions with at least two neighbors. Conversation was an integral part of any Raeford shopping experience, and I had often accompanied my mother on the same walk to Mr. Harrell's store.

Ms. Lilly Brown would pretend she was doing yard work, although it was obvious that she never actually tended anything in that wild thicket of a yard. Yard work was her excuse to keep an eye on things in the neighborhood and chat with any passersby. I always prayed that Lilly's son, Pete, wasn't with her. Pete Brown lived with his mother at the age of 40, and while some folks considered him mentally challenged, I knew his behavior was the result of the massive quantities of alcohol that Pete consumed. His withered physical appearance frightened me almost more than anything I heard or saw in my house or basement – almost.

Ms. Faulk's house was across the street, and she lived in her upstairs window. One minute Ms. Faulk would be in the window and the next minute she would appear right behind you. Although she looked to be about 114, she was quick on her feet and always spoke directly into your face without bothering to insert her teeth. She would keep my mother talking for at least 15 minutes, so on this particular sunny day, I knew I had enough time for my first exploration.

Without any further consideration, I inserted the key into the lock on the off-limits basement door, thereby risking a whipping with the razor strap that my father favored as a means of punishment. He himself had felt the bite of its damaging whips as a challenging child, and he apparently wanted to continue the tradition.

Despite the possible consequences, I turned the key and ventured into the unknown – changing my life forever.

Inky blackness immediately engulfed me, and I had to retrieve the flashlight that was always atop the mantle next to the fancy purple goblet. As I walked away from the basement entrance and back into the living room, I could feel an unmistakable coldness follow me out of the basement.

Armed with the flashlight, I proceeded carefully down the basement steps that let out the familiar creaking sound I had heard my father make so many times on his trips up and down. There was no railing to hold, so I walked carefully and counted the 13 steps out loud.

At the bottom, a concrete wall and a wooden ramp led to a mysterious doorway as the smell of death closed in around me and the temperature dropped with each step.

Wooden planks acted as makeshift bridges that lead to various chambers of the basement. The low, dirt floor of the basement held about an inch of dirty water. I never learned where the water came from, but I knew that stepping into the muddy moisture would be a dead giveaway of my whereabouts, so I stayed carefully on the wooden planks.

I saw a shimmer of light shining from underneath one door and knew that it led outside. Another door, marked "Do Not Enter" was to my right.

It was heavy and resistant, but eventually opened far enough to reveal the embalming room. It was in a higher part of the basement, and had a dry concrete floor. The things I saw froze me in my place even as an overpowering stench assaulted my senses.

My fear mixed with the smell of death that hung heavy in the air as my gaze landed on a giant sink and other items near it. Huge jars looked to be filled with blood, and test tubes hung from a bracket on the wall.

Large scalpels were lined up next to the sink, their sharpened blades massive to my 10-year-old eyes. The floor was concrete, sending its cold into my body through my shoes.

That's when I noticed the oversized drain in the dead center of the room with a long white slab standing over it, and blood stains all around it. One round thick metal leg was inserted in the belly of the slab and was permanently affixed to the concrete floor.

A machine that resembled a large mixer was against the far wall, plugged into an oddly shaped outlet. Bloodstained white cabinets lined the wall with large fishing hooks hanging beneath them.

As I looked closer, I noticed that the ceiling and walls were also soiled with their share of blood. I had entered the chamber of Frankenstein, but in that moment, I came to the gruesome conclusion that my father was the monster.

I quickly shut the door and headed back toward the stairs. My body was having a physical reaction to what I had seen, and I didn't know if I was going to wet my pants or throw up. But I did know I had to get away from the embalming room as fast as my feet would carry me. I remember dropping the flashlight and panicking as I scratched around for it in the thick blackness.

Finally I found it and continued my retreat. During my exit I caught a glimpse of another wooden ramp over dark water. That plank led in a different direction, toward another unmarked door, but at that moment my only thought was escape. I had to get out of the basement.

My little body was numb and I stumbled on two of the stairs, but finally, breathlessly, reached the top of the staircase. It was then that I heard what sounded like a baby's cry coming from the basement, but I couldn't bring myself to look back. I managed to open the door and get to the safe haven of my familiar, upstairs home as beads of sweat poured off my head and my hands shook uncontrollably.

I locked the door and returned the key to the purple goblet on the mantle. My timing was perfect, and I was putting the mourner's chair back in place as my mother appeared at the front door.

She said I looked awfully pale, and asked if I was feeling poorly. I dared not tell her of my gruesome discovery. I knew I had no business being in the forbidden basement, and I would not return to the macabre chamber of death for several years.

But my first discovery of the embalming room had lasting effects. The sound of a child's cry would continue unabated in my head or in my home, and from that day on, all my dreams were nightmares.

CHAPTER 9
No Medical Explanation

That first trip to the basement changed me forever, and I've thought a lot about how different my life would have been if I had stayed away from that underground nightmare.

I couldn't concentrate in school, and then I suffered a series of four seizures. One occurred in the school lunchroom. My eyes rolled back in my head and I was unresponsive until I eventually lost consciousness and passed out.

After the fourth collapse, my father took me to the hospital, convinced that I had a brain tumor or some other neurological problem.

I spent 12 weeks in the children's ward of the hospital, and underwent more tests, both physical and psychological, than I care to remember.

There were spinal taps and EKG's. The nurses had to shave part of my head to attach some adhesive circles with wires streaming out of them. A Pakistani neurologist named Dr. Muhammad asked me all sorts of questions, and my father came to see me every day, asking me more questions and demanding that the doctors find out what was wrong with me.

I finally told the psychologists about the voices and noises I heard in our house. I told them about the ghosts that I saw. I told them all this because I needed someone to know the truth. I needed someone to believe me. But most of all,

I needed someone to tell me I was normal even though I wasn't.

I also knew that I was safe from my father's strap as long as I was in the hospital, so I felt more comfortable talking about Phyllis and the others.

Psychologists asked me whether my head hurt when I saw these visions. They asked where I was in the house when I heard things, and they asked what the voices said to me. In hindsight, I wonder if the doctors, during my 12-week evaluation, eventually realized they were dealing with an abused child. Nowadays, I would assume they would have to notify authorities of any suspicions they had. But in the 1970s, people didn't go around accusing fathers of beating their daughters. They saw a devoted father visiting his daughter every day, and occasionally bringing my mother to visit. They saw only what they wanted to.

When he released me from the hospital, Dr. Mohammad told my father that there was "no medical explanation" for what I saw and heard. I did not have a brain tumor or other neurological condition that would produce visual and auditory hallucinations.

Such a diagnosis would have made things easier for me. Instead, I simply felt crazy. And my father did little to comfort me, despite the fact that all of my symptoms mirrored those that his own mother, my namesake, experienced throughout much of her life.

My father never mentioned the similarities, and instead insisted on my silence about ghosts, visions and crossing over. After all, a ranting child was not good for the funeral home business.

But I knew something had happened during my trip to the basement, and I knew things continued to happen. I knew what I saw and I knew what I heard.

My father constantly threatened to call Dorothy Dix Mental Hospital and have me committed if I continued talking about ghosts. I lived in fear of the mental hospital, and so I vowed to remain silent about what I saw in the funeral home.

I kept quiet, and started sleeping with a night light. To this day, I cannot go to bed without one.

CHAPTER 10
A Gruesome Education

By the time I entered middle school, classmates had started inquiring about my father's bizarre profession and the macabre embalming process. I didn't know the answers to their questions, and actually had to look up the words "embalming" and "undertaker" in the dictionary.

I had no clue what my father did to prepare people to meet their Maker, but I desperately wanted to fit in with my peers at Upchurch Junior High, so I had to find answers.

I had been trying unsuccessfully to fit in since nursery school. Throughout grade school, I was just the strange girl who lived in a funeral home, had a hearse in the driveway and bodies in the basement. After fourth grade, I was "that girl" whose eyes had rolled back in her skull, and who had collapsed in the cafeteria.

Such stories, nicknames, rumors and lies follow a student in a small town. By the time I reached middle school, everyone knew who I was, but few wanted to be my friend.

I remember walking along the same route that other kids took to and from school in hopes of establishing a friendship. The route took us past a sand pile that led to the top of the bridge over Highway 211. The bridge and sand pile were a popular hang-out.

After reaching the top, a few kids would proclaim themselves "king of the bridge," and only allow certain other people at the top of the pile. More than anything, I wanted to climb up that bridge and sit with them, and I remember the day one local boy told me I could join them – but only if I shared the details of my father's embalming process. In that moment of middle-school angst, I made it my mission to learn more about what took place in our basement.

My education began in eighth grade when I found a manual in my father's briefcase. I had not returned to the basement since fourth grade, and after the shock of that visit, reading seemed a much safer way to get more information.

But I had no idea what I was about to learn. The book provided graphic photos of the embalming process, and step-by-step details of the tasks my father performed in our basement.

First, the body was shaved from the neck down to the toes except for the head and facial hair. The book also said that a dead body releases excessive odors, so the undertaker would make several incisions into the body to stave off decomposition and release excess gases.

One incision was made just above the clavicle near the carotid artery. Another ran along the inner thigh at the femoral artery. The hooks I saw in the basement were not for fishing. I learned that the undertaker used them to hold open the human tissue while he drained the blood and injected embalming fluid. He used the scalpels I saw to cut the veins and arteries and then insert test tubes of fluid inside the body. The undertaker pumped embalming fluid, which is made of formaldehyde and alcohol, into the arteries while he applied vascular pressure to the body, forcing the blood to shoot out of the veins. I immediately realized that an embalming room would be a vampire's dream, and understood where all the blood in our basement had come from.

Once the required amount of blood has been removed from the body, another dose of embalming fluid is injected, and a hollow tube is inserted into the lower right part of the belly to drain any remaining bodily liquids. My adolescent mind was amused to learn that a dead person can still pass gas, an act referred to as a snart. It is considered a toxic gas and is said to be hazardous to a person's health.

I also learned that the undertaker had some hidden talents. He knew how to sew, as he had to close all the incisions that he made and put the body back together with a large needle and thick thread. He also washed and styled the hair of dead people, and then dressed them, from the waist up, in their Sunday best.

The last thing my father did was apply heavy foundation and makeup in an effort to bring a lifelike color back to the otherwise pale and bloodless face.

After the embalming and grooming process was completed, the undertaker manipulated the body into a posed position.

The book had explained a lot, and I now knew the purpose of all the items in our basement, including the drain in the middle of the floor, which collected the blood and other fluids. I have often wondered where that drain led, as there were few water treatment plants back in those days.

Nowadays it's common for the drains in funeral homes to be flushed into a local sewer system and end up in a treatment plant. Since the blood is mixed with the embalming chemicals during that whole process, it is supposed to be safe and free of disease. Some undertakers claim to add an additional disinfectant chemical before they flush the fluids into the drain basin. The disposal of blood and body fluids in this manner is approved by the Environmental Protection Agency, but it should come as no surprise that to this day I don't drink water from a faucet and I rarely eat meat.

CHAPTER 11
High School Hijinks

My four years at Hoke County High School were difficult, and I faced more problems than most adolescents struggling with their changing bodies, raging hormones and fierce need for acceptance. My mother did not drive and I would not have a car until I was 21 and living on my own in Florida. Fortunately my neighbor and fellow ghost-sighter, Lisa Crowder, was a senior who gave me a ride to school every morning. As with most teenage girls, boys became my main focus.

Back then, a good Southern Friday night meant sitting in the parking lot of Mack's five and dime. A car full of girls would park in the lot and watch the boys of our town cruise the town's main street.

On Saturday night, bonfires burned at Rock Fish Creek on the outskirts of town. On Sundays, we'd jump off Twin Bridges into a frigid creek while partaking of the usual adolescent vices of cigarettes, beer and marijuana, or rabbit tobacco, as my mother called it. When she told me that, I hadn't realized that pot had been around for so long.

By high school, I had made a few friends, or at least acquaintances. We'd go out on a Friday or Saturday night, and I'd throw back a couple of cold Budweisers and hit a joint or two before asking someone for a ride home to the morgue. I was always hoping the numbing combination of pot and alcohol would drown out the sounds and cries, which, by then, I was hearing constantly.

Now that I am older, I don't drink alcohol or smoke marijuana. In fact I rarely leave my house after dark. It's funny how life changes us. Most of us eventually grow up emotionally. We spend half of our life trying to get away from where we came from, and the other half trying to reconnect with it.

Things had been looking up for me prior to my sophomore year of high school. Near the end of my freshman year in high school, I had tried out for the junior varsity cheerleading squad and made the team. I still don't know where I got the courage to audition, but it was one of the happiest times in my life. I was finally turning into a somewhat attractive young lady and was letting my hair grow longer after years of having the undertaker cut it by placing a bowl over the top of my head.

As a way to further exert his control over my mother and me, my father steadfastly refused to let me date. One boy finally got up the nerve to ask me out, knowing that when it was over, he would have to walk me to the darkened doorway of the funeral home around midnight.

In the end it didn't matter because my father said I couldn't go.

My few friends would often step in and help me deceive

him. We'd say I was spending the night at a friend's house, and then have the whole night to drive around, often ending up sneaking into bars and flirting with soldiers from Fort Bragg.

They were often fascinated by my father's profession and my life in a funeral home. They were also interested in the chemicals the undertaker used to stave off decomposition.

I remember one group of guys constantly trying to convince me to sell them some of my father's embalming fluid. They said they wanted to spray it on their pot for a better high. I had no idea whether it would actually work, but I knew that in order to fulfill their request I would have to return to the basement embalming room, and that was not a journey I was prepared to take.

But marijuana was something I knew a little about, so I was able to recognize the plants that were growing on the Cox's wooded property near my house.

I harvested pot from about 50 or 60 plants, and decided to bake it in my mother's oven. Our kitchen was located one floor above the funeral home, and it was always empty when my parents were busy with a service.

I lined the pot on a baking sheet and turned on the oven, not realizing that the aroma of "rabbit tobacco" soon would fill the whole house. Although the smell was familiar to me and all of my peers, many adults did not recognize it, and they assumed the pleasant, earthy aroma was coming from one of the funeral floral arrangements.

I have to say, there was more laughter during that service than any other I remember – and more food consumed after the ceremony. I had unwittingly given the entire gathering a contact high, and no one was ever the wiser. If my mom had her suspicions, she never let on, obviously saving us both a severe beating.

CHAPTER 12
Winter Hawk Hell

It was early spring of my sophomore year when the strange and terrifying noises at my house became unbearable. The most frustrating part was that I was still the only person who heard them.

I awoke one night in a cold sweat and could not fall back to sleep. Lying in bed with the glow of a night light nearby, I heard a loud cry, accompanied by the groan of what could only be a dying person. The cry echoed below the hall floor furnace and was different from the usual sounds of people whispering and doors slamming that I had grown accustomed to hearing at night. The shadowy forms of the dead didn't seem to faze me anymore, but this cry was human to some degree and seemed all too normal – too alive, and it grew louder each night as summer approached.

I knew from an early age that no one else saw or heard things in our house. What was the point of speaking to my parents about these experiences? I would get beaten, and possibly locked up in a nuthouse. It was bad enough that no kids would spend the night at our house. I didn't want my high school years to be like my childhood years.

June was always my favorite month, because it brought my Aunt Edna up from Florida for a weeklong visit. She always stayed in a hotel in Fayetteville with her two grandchildren, and I was always allowed to sleep in the hotel with them. It was the only week of the year that I would sleep uninterrupted and in peace, so I hated to see her return to Florida, as it meant my return to the funeral home.

My first night home that June, the cries resumed, forcing me to put a pillow over my head. But nothing would drown out the awful groans.

I had tried a few times to return to the basement to investigate its source but I always froze in place in front of the crystal doorknob.

The nights were endless. I was so tired and confused, and I felt like I was a crazy person pretending to be sane. My parents continued to claim that they never heard noises.

In August I decided I had to venture back into that place of darkness. School was going to start and I was already living on auto pilot. I would be kicked off the cheerleading squad if my grades dropped and practices were the only place I felt like a normal teen-aged girl.

It was a hot August night and the lack of sleep had been taking its toll. I was having trouble retaining the new cheers, and nothing I tried would help me sleep. The nightly cries always woke me and kept me up all night. I was on the verge of a mental breakdown and I could not take the insanity anymore.

There was only one thing to do; one terrifying thing.

I had to return to the basement and find out why those cries were filling my head. On this next attempt, I didn't freeze at the basement door. The atmosphere in the funeral home was different this night. It was as if the door unlocked itself for me. I do not recall retrieving the key from the purple goblet on the mantle, but I know the cries intensified with each step I took down that wooden staircase.

As I descended, flashbacks from my first and last fifth-grade trip to the basement replayed in my mind. That misadventure had landed me in the mental hospital. Sure, I was deemed sane, but only a crazy person would still be hearing voices, and decide to return to this place of darkness. Was I crazy or actually tapping into another dimension that some people call the Nether World?

The Pakistani doctor had mentioned this possibility even while he was telling my father that my condition was medically unexplainable. And the undertaker continued to threaten me, saying that if I ever told anyone again what I had seen, he would have me committed to the Dorothy Dix Mental Health Facility.

He said I was destroying everything he had worked so hard to build and to keep my mouth shut.

Yet there I was heading back down those stairs as if pulled by a magnetic force. I never hesitated or flinched.

As I approached the bottom of the staircase, there was an unusual light to my left. This was not a normal ray of light and I only have seen it twice. The light seemed to beckon and then it led me to a dead baby lying in the dirt.

The tiny form seemed to have wings made of feathers, and when I looked away from the baby, the light disappeared. The room was once again in complete darkness.

The last thing I recall was waking up in my bed. Had I gone down into the basement or was it just a dream?

Sometimes early in life we are presented with unexplainable circumstances. For me, this was just one more in a series of bizarre incidents. I would become obsessed with the dead child I chose to call Winter Hawk.

Where did Winter Hawk come from? How long had Winter Hawk been in the basement? I had to have answers. I had to return to the basement.

I knew not to mention the situation to the undertaker. The basement was off limits, so I had to time my visit carefully. I left cheerleading practice early on a day I knew both parents would be out of the house.

By 1979, we had a telephone answering machine so it was no longer necessary for someone to be home at all times. But I knew my mom never stayed out for more than two hours, so I would have to make the most of my time on this third expedition to the basement. I retrieved the skeleton key and put fresh batteries in the flashlight. It was daylight, but the funeral home appeared dark at any hour.

As I slowly opened the basement door, the stink of death once again filled the room. I gasped for my breath and began my descent with each step, the temperature dropped and the odor intensified. When I reached the bottom of the staircase, I turned left to find the wooden plank that led to the next doorway. I pointed the flashlight toward the ground, again discovering that dirty black water that surrounded all sides of the makeshift bridge. I didn't know how deep it was or why it was in the basement. The surroundings reminded me of an underground cave. The smell of death combined with the water stench was overwhelming.

Finally after walking the short ramp, I reached the entrance to another room. My feet felt like they were frozen and I thought they might be wet. I pointed the flashlight downward and noticed the water was gone. The ground was again black dirt. I found myself in a huge vertical room with a cold dirt floor. The walls were concrete. It reminded me of a dungeon.

Had the undertaker created this room before I was born? The town rumors about the mysterious undertaker and his refusal to accept help when moving in, were consuming my thoughts. I walked to my left and again heard the baby cry. I looked down and was shocked to find the badly decomposed remains of a child. Here was Winter Hawk, just like in my premonition.

I ran out of the entrance and over the ramp. I scurried up the staircase and quickly shut the door. The baby's cry intensified in my head, and would remain until Winter Hawk could be put to rest.

How was I going to get the cries out of my head? I knew the child needed to cross over and was calling on me for help. The cries grew louder and louder as each second passed. I felt so alone knowing there was no one I could tell about my discovery. Even if I could speak of this day, would anyone believe me?

I had reached my final breaking point as the cries replayed in my head 24 hours a day. Shortly thereafter, I remember going to the Highway 211 bridge about a mile from the funeral home. It was the same one I had wanted to climb throughout middle school. This time, I put on my best Sunday clothes and high heels.

I climbed to the top and stood on the bridge rail in those high heels. I looked down on the town of Raeford and wondered why I was the only one who heard these mysterious things. Was it me or was it the house? Why did the house have a dungeon down below? Was the undertaker the one who was crazy? Does it really matter?

An unfamiliar presence greeted me as I stood on the bridge railing. It told me I was not like everyone else. Time seemed to stand still, and I did not know how much time had passed. It was if I were in a trance.

There I stood on the rail in my high heels at the age of 15. What do I do about Winter Hawk? The presence told me I already knew.

I am still not sure how long I stood on the bridge that day. I remember someone from the local sheriff's office convincing me to come down. I came out of the trance and noticed there were numerous bystanders gathered on the bridge. I remember stepping off the rails and seeing the undertaker waiting at the bottom. He was furious.

And as expected, when we got home he called Dorothy Dix Mental Ward. I knew my days of freedom were limited and I also knew what must be done.

I was locked in my bedroom and not allowed out. An appointment had been made for an evaluation in three days.

A thunderstorm was raging the evening I climbed out my bedroom window and headed for the Mack's five and dime parking lot to convince a classmate to come to my basement with me. To this day, I still can't believe anyone agreed to accompany me, and I shudder to think of how crazed I appeared that night.

I was desperate and thought that if I could show what I had seen to someone else, then it would prove there were ghosts in the basement. On the other hand, it could also prove I was totally crazy.

I had watched the undertaker place a key underneath a brick at the back of the house on the outside. It was how he got into the embalming room without going through the house. I found the key and remembered there was a flashlight in the hearse. There was no way to go into the basement without some type of light.

My classmate was choking with every step we took into the basement. The scent of death filled our lungs like toxic poison. Traveling through the darkness of the basement morgue, we finally reached the remains of Winter Hawk. When my girlfriend saw the baby's decomposed body, she let out a terrifying scream. It seemed like the dungeon walls were shaking and the dirt floor was buckling. We quickly ran out of the room. When we exited the little basement door, my classmate ran off into the darkness.

I climbed up on the pile of bricks that were placed outside my bedroom window to allow my escape. The lightning cracked and thunder roared as if the funeral home had gone mad. I managed to get back up and close the bedroom window, thinking the scream had certainly awakened my mother, but the sound of the thunder apparently prevailed.

My father would have been sleeping, as usual, at the antique shop, so he would not have heard my girlfriend's scream.

A knock came at the door a few hours later, and I remember my mother unlocking my bedroom door to tell me that Chief Wiggins was downstairs. Apparently someone had called the sheriff's department to report a dead baby in our basement. At that moment, the undertaker drove up behind the squad cars that surrounded our house.

He escorted the police into the basement, where they too, were greeted with the scent of death. I knew immediately that they took Winter Hawk with them because the baby's cries finally stopped. I was filled with a peace that made me cry.

CHAPTER 13
Violent Consequences

The peace I felt when Winter Hawk was silenced did not last long, for I had done the unthinkable and involved other people in my father's private affairs.

I had told people about a decomposing baby in our basement, and described the cries that I heard every night despite my father's warning to remain silent.

He beat my mother and me to within an inch of our lives in the wake of the Winter Hawk incident. It was the worst violence I had experienced at my father's hands, and then I had to watch my mother suffer for my actions.

She stayed inside for more than a week, waiting for the swelling to go down and the bruises to fade enough to be covered with makeup. An intense hatred toward my father simmered inside me as I watched him hit my mother relentlessly and with a ferocity that was no longer human.

This was more than the short-lived tantrums we had endured for years. This was an explosion, a letting loose of all that was wrong in his world. It was as if he was punishing us for being alive, and for ruining whatever life he had envisioned for himself as a graduate of Randolph-Macon Academy.

The beatings we suffered after the Winter Hawk incident were the worst we had ever experienced, but they were also the last.

My grades had been plummeting since the breakdown on the bridge, the sleepless nights filled with a baby's screams and the subsequent discovery of a decomposing infant in our basement. I really couldn't blame myself for a few missed assignments. I had other things on my mind, to say the least.

A guidance counselor eventually called me in to her office for a chat. She wanted to know about my sliding grades, and about the long-sleeved shirts that had become a wardrobe staple in the weeks since the drama unfolded. The counselors had tried to speak with me about my home life on other occasions, but I was always able to dodge them and avoid the inevitable questions.

Raeford was a small town with few secrets, and I'm convinced that the violence in our home was not a well-kept secret. The Crowder family next door knew what went on, and Mrs. Crowder always let me spend time at their house.

But domestic violence was not discussed in the 1970s. People minded their own business, and refused to rock the boat. No one wanted to get involved, and whatever Jim Lentz did behind closed doors was of no concern to them.

Occasionally, a concerned teacher would furrow her brow after noticing the bruises on an arm I accidentally revealed when rolling up my sleeves in class. But if anyone asked any questions, or wanted to talk to me about things, I quickly changed the subject and assured them all was well at home.

Fortunately or unfortunately, no one seemed eager to press the issue. I tried the same avoidance tactic on that particular day, and when the counselor asked about any problems at home, I told her I didn't want to talk about it and tugged my long sleeves past my fingers.

But there was no way to cover my bare legs, and the counselor gasped in horror when she saw the swollen bruises and cuts along the backs of them. I suppose one look in my eyes told her all she needed to know and prompted an immediate call to the county's social services division.

The social workers picked me up from school that day so I wouldn't have to face the wrath of a violent father whose secrets had been exposed. I remember the woman who became my case manager because she insisted I call her by her first name, Chris. She was new in town, and didn't care how well-respected my father was. She didn't have any political favors to repay, and she was not afraid to expose a pillar of the community for the two-faced monster he could be.

I learned later that my father was livid when he learned what had happened. I shuddered to think of him, in my absence, unleashing that fury on my mother. But the intervention by social services would also be her salvation.

The social workers dropped me off at the modest home of

a minister and his wife. Their name now escapes me, but they were a very nice couple with no children of their own, or at least none who still lived at home. Their house was about five miles from the funeral home, but I was not allowed to see my parents for three months, as we waited for our day in court.

I remember once again sleeping the sleep of the dead – no pun intended – the whole time I was away from home. It was the same peaceful sleep I enjoyed in the hotel every summer when my aunt would visit.

On the day of our court hearing, Chris picked me up at the minister's house and drove me to the Hoke County Courthouse, where I would see my father for the first time since I revealed his abusive nature.

We were led into the judge's private chambers, where I saw my parents, the judge and a few others whom I now realize must have been lawyers and a court reporter.

Chris stayed in the room with me while the judge asked me questions about my home life. For the first time in my life, I let the words of truth tumble from my mouth like a waterfall.

I told the judge and social workers about the beatings, the razor strap and the threats to send me to a mental hospital. I told them about my father's tantrums, about hiding in the woods with my mother, and about the things I saw and heard in our house.

Then it was my mother's turn to talk. The judge turned his attention to my meek and terrified mother and asked her about the beatings – right in front of my father.

Not surprisingly, my mother denied everything while my father stared across the table at her. She told the judge that her husband had never laid a hand on her, and said that she was unaware of anything he had done to me.

At one point during the hearing, the judge asked my father to leave the room, and questioned my mother again. But she still didn't break.

LaRue Brennan Lentz lied through her teeth to protect the man who would have knocked those teeth out – if the damage wouldn't have been so visible to the rest of the town.

Her silence crushed me. We were no longer in this together. I was on my own; an awkward teen-ager with a history of mental instability facing an elected official, a Mason, a member of the Moose Lodge and a trusted funeral director.

At this point, I realized my mother was incapable of such resolve and lacked the courage to stand up to her husband. I also realized that any beating I avoided would inevitably land on her. She still needed protection and

I couldn't provide it if I was sleeping soundly at the minister's house five miles away.

I told the judge that I would return home, as long as my father swore not to touch my mother or me again. The judge looked at him, and my father nodded solemnly before telling the judge that he had never, and would never hit his wife or child.

When presented with photographic evidence of my cuts and bruises, my father told the judge that he believed the marks "were of my own doing."

I'll never know whether it was love, fear or a bizarre combination of the two that prompted my mother to protect my father. But as it turned out, I had said enough for both of us.

My father never laid a hand on us again.

When I returned home, he explained the presence of Winter Hawk in our basement by reminding me that he had bought our house – and all the contents of the old McDiarmid Funeral Home – in 1947. He apparently never thoroughly inventoried the items he had received from McDiarmid, because it was 1955 by the time he uncovered the baby's remains in a forgotten wooden crate in that secret subterranean room.

At the time, my father was also the county coroner. He had been appointed to the position in 1948 when his predecessor died in office. He served out the remaining term of the late W.L. Roper before running for the office in 1950 as the incumbent coroner. He was elected in 1950 and again in 1954.

My father was well acquainted with the state's burial laws, and he told me that burials in those days required a permit, and such permits required a family member's signature. My father insisted that he had tried at the time to get a permit but was denied by North Carolina state authorities because there was no relative to approve it. No one knew who the child was or the whereabouts of the family.

An article about the baby's remains appeared in the local newspaper soon after the authorities removed it from our basement. The article prompted someone to finally claim Winter Hawk. Apparently, Caroline Purcell was with child when she died in January 1936. Her unborn baby also died and was removed from the womb but never buried. Family members wrongly assumed the child was buried in the casket with the mother. The child had been in the basement of my house, Lentz Mortuary, since the 1940s. Winter Hawk was finally laid to rest in 1979.

I wrote the following poem about Winter Hawk in November of that year:

"Winter Hawk with soaring feathers white and wide, which direction would you choose to glide?
Will your travel be far or near, and what will be your unconquerable destiny as you leave here?
Will you fly high to mighty heaven and there dwell?
Will you change your defeated course and go to a fiery hell?
What will be the emerging path you take as you leave this wild blue yonder like a feather floating away?
When your long, tiresome journey finally comes to an end, I wonder if there will be another winter hawk to pick up where you began."

By the time I was 16, my father had stopped beating us, and he had a plausible explanation for the dead baby in our basement. But he made no attempt to explain the manmade dungeon under our house, and he still wouldn't acknowledge the things I had heard and seen. I didn't dare mention either of the topics, but was simply glad the child's tortured cries had stopped. For once, I simply enjoyed the silence in my head and the relative calm in our house.

CHAPTER 14
Starting Over

I wasted no time leaving Raeford or the funeral home. I kept my promise to myself and moved to Fort Lauderdale, Florida the very day I graduated from high school in 1981.

I was 18 and had been waiting decades for the chance to leave behind not only my small town and inexplicable home, but the whole state of North Carolina.

My father and I were barely on speaking terms by the time I left, so there were no tearful goodbyes. It had been years since we had enjoyed the happier times of my childhood: the trips to collect burial insurance, the hunt for Christmas trees and the unexpected thank-you gift of a pet rooster.

The usual father-teenaged daughter disagreements had disintegrated into an estranged relationship due to his continued refusal to believe what I told him about what I had seen and heard in our house. That, and of course, the violence that had permanently scarred my childhood.

I was gone for five years before my father came to see me in Florida - to walk me down the aisle at my wedding. He tried desperately during that visit to make amends, and finally told me that he believed everything I had seen and heard. But by then, it was too late and I refused to listen.

Years then passed without any communication between us. The undertaker would tell anyone who asked that he was in touch with me, and that I was doing well in Florida.

He had tried to get in touch; tried to make things better, but I refused to answer his letters or return his calls. Too much had happened. He had put me through too much and, in my mind, he didn't deserve my correspondence. He didn't deserve my forgiveness. He was all but dead to me after I left North Carolina, and it remained that way for 11 years.

But one jarring phone call on Christmas Day in 1992 changed everything, and peace was borne of tragedy.

The call was from the Fayetteville/Cape Fear Valley Hospital, and the Southern accent on the other end of the line told me my father had been shot seven times and was not expected to survive.

I packed immediately and headed for North Carolina on that Christmas Day, when it seemed that death would once again rob me of a holiday.

I had made yearly trips back to Carolina after relocating. I had gone regularly to see my mother at Sun Bridge Rest Home in Elizabethtown, and would visit my grandmother's home in White Oak.

My mother had moved back to White Oak, North Carolina, shortly after I left town. It's where she was born and raised, and her family was still there. By the time she moved, she was completely blind in one eye, and had only minimal vision in her other "good" eye.

My father had accrued a good amount of debt, much of which stemmed from my constant claims of ghosts and visions, which were not good for the funeral business. He sold the house on West Prospect Avenue and moved to Fayetteville. Although they lived apart for the rest of their lives, my parents never divorced.

Both of them eventually went blind, and I firmly believe that the things they saw in the basement cost them their vision. We once had a family dog that stayed in the basement much of the time so as not to mess up the funeral home or disturb any services. The dog also went blind.

During the long drive north on that Christmas Day, while my father lay in a hospital bed with seven gunshot wounds, I thought of my early childhood and of the life lessons he had taught me. I recalled the Christmas when he gave that poor family a tree and presents, and I thought of how he never judged people based on their skin color, despite our location in the racially divided South.

It's funny, I didn't think about the ghosts, the razor strap, our disagreements or the visions and sounds I had grown up with. I did indeed have some terrible memories but there were also times when my father demonstrated his love for me.

These instances came to the forefront of my mind during

that momentous road trip that resulted in reconciliation. Despite the years of bizarre behavior, I knew the undertaker loved me and I loved him. For the first time, I prayed that my creator would allow the good in me to see the good in him.

When I got to the hospital, a minister was waiting in the hallway. I found the wounded undertaker and held his hand, suddenly wondering why I had spent so many years ignoring him. I realized that we get no rewards for being right in this world, and I didn't need anyone to confirm what I had seen in the funeral home. How important was the past anyway?

As I sat and held my father's hand that night in the hospital, I wondered what he would have said if I had, just once, picked up the phone. I felt the answer without truly hearing it. The answer was, "I love you and don't look back. Look where we are right now, my daughter."

I squeezed his hand tightly and let the love from my heart pass from me to the old man dying before my tired eyes. Who was I to have judged him for all those years?

Perception is a unique thing. People don't always see the same things, and the fact that I don't see something doesn't mean it's not there. I realized then and there that some of us can tap into things others cannot. I don't ask, "Why me?" anymore, but rather, "Why not me?"

The undertaker miraculously recovered despite one bullet that remained inside him, too close to major organs for doctors to remove. After a few weeks he was able to tell me about the Christmas Eve shooting. He had picked up a hitchhiker, who robbed him and then shot him seven times in the chest before leaving him to die in a ditch. An army soldier from Fort Bragg somehow discovered my father and called the authorities.

The following article about the shooting appeared in the "Fayetteville Observer" in December of 1992:

"A Fayetteville man was shot several times after he picked up a hitchhiker early Sunday, according to the Cumberland County Sheriff's Department. James C. Lentz, 67, of 107 Woodside Avenue told deputies that he picked up a hitchhiker on Bragg Boulevard and traveled to Raeford Road at about 4 a.m. Sunday. The hitchhiker pulled a small pistol and shot Mr. Lentz several times causing him to wreck his car on a dirt road near an overpass on Raeford Road, according to the sheriff's department report. Mr. Lentz was listed in serious condition Sunday night at Cape Fear Valley Medical Center, a hospital spokesman said."

CHAPTER 15
Confirmation at Last

My tumultuous childhood in the funeral home and estranged relationship with my father had prompted me to seek mental health therapy after leaving Raeford. I eventually learned that no matter how many shrinks told me I wasn't crazy, the only people I wanted to hear it from were my parents.

My father lived for eight years after the shooting – long enough for us to make amends and establish a healthy, loving relationship. I believe the undertaker survived the shooting to allow us to reconnect. This book would not have been created without our happy reunion, and my father eventually confirmed what I had seen in the funeral home, and said he regretted not being able to tell me years prior.

All families have their secrets but the undertaker finally acknowledged everything that went on in that house. He knew I wasn't lying. He told me that my grandmother, for whom I was named, had a similar gift of intuition, psychic powers, or anything else you wanted to call it.

He told me that his own mother always knew when he had been doing something wrong. She had seen ghosts and spirits, and she had experienced premonitions and other phenomena.

My father knew I didn't have any imaginary friends, and he knew I had the same intuition as his mother. The Pakistani doctor couldn't provide a medical explanation for our condition, but acknowledged that some people simply saw things and felt things and knew things that couldn't be explained by science.

My father knew all this, but he also knew that the funeral home was his only means of providing for me, and he couldn't run a funeral home with a lunatic daughter running around claiming she saw ghosts rise from their coffins in our living room.

But my father ultimately admitted to having seen his share of ghosts and other inexplicable occurrences. He never heard the voices or noises that I heard, but he saw things that he dared not discuss.

I struggled for many years with the things I saw as a child, but I eventually understood why my father didn't – couldn't – acknowledge them. There were no manuals for parenting back then, and certainly no how-to guides for explaining ghosts, apparitions, premonitions and overwhelming intuition.

My father sat in his room at Raeford Manor Rest Home in October 2000 and told me that you do the best you can with what you have and hope your child has a better life than you. I don't think he ever realized just how damaged I was from all of the abuse until then. I would like to believe that the undertaker would have done things differently had he been given another chance.

CHAPTER 16

The Undertaker's Funeral

The undertaker resided at Raeford Manor Rest Home at the end of his life. The years had taken their toll, and he needed round-the-clock care. After so many years of separation between us, everything had finally come full circle, and we reconciled our past and reconnected in the present.

We had discussed his death, and the undertaker did not want to be cremated. He had witnessed a cremation during his years in the industry and had never forgotten the smell of a human body burning at 1,500 degrees. He told me of the cremation that he and other undertakers attended. A woman's body was being lowered with chains into the oven, and my father swears he and the others heard the scream as her soul left the body.

The undertaker begged me not to cremate him, and I promised to honor his wishes on one condition: he had to make amends with my mother and seek her forgiveness for the life he forced her to endure.

He agreed, and during one of my trips to North Carolina, I picked up my mother at Sun Bridge Rest Home in Elizabethtown and drove her the two hours to Raeford Manor.

She had suffered a stroke and was unable to speak, but she answered questions with her eyes: one blink for yes and two for no.

From his room at Raeford Manor, my father looked my mother in the eye and apologized – for everything. He said he was sorry for the things he did, and the things he didn't do, for the husband he was and for the man that he wasn't.

And when he finally asked my mother if she could ever forgive him, she blinked once. I took a photo that day of my mother leaning over my father's bed.

It was the last photo taken of my father, who died December 15, 2000. I picked out his casket and attire, as he had done for more than 1,000 people, and I thought of all the flower arrangements he had created, and of all the people he had prepared to meet their Maker.

Now it was his turn, and Dr. John Ropp, the minister with whom I shared a birthday and a special connection, said the final words for the undertaker. The hymns were not like those I heard during the funerals of my childhood. Instead, we sang Christmas carols. It was still my favorite time of the year, and it held some of the best memories I had of my father.

I buried my father in the Raeford cemetery, where his gravestone reads "Those are not lost who find the light of sun and stars and God. May you rest in peace, Dad."

The verse was the same that had been uttered at the funeral for my grandmother who had provided me with my name as well as her indescribable ability to see, hear and feel the other world. I found the scripture passage among the undertaker's personal belongings, and have since been asked numerous times about its origins, as those who read it seem to find comfort in its simplicity.

My mother died nine years after my father, also in December. It was 2009 and she had been living for years at the Sun Bridge Rest Home in Elizabethtown, N.C.

I was still living in Florida when I got the call about her death, and my son and I left immediately for North Carolina.

Upon arrival, my aunt took me to Gaskins funeral home to view my mother privately. I knew the routine. A family member must approve everything before friends can begin to pay their respects. But my familiarity with the process did not make it any easier to say to good-bye to my last living parent. And as an only child, at 46 years old, I suddenly felt truly alone in the world.

Before the wave of panic, despair and loneliness enveloped me completely, I experienced a wave of utter comfort and confidence.

I will never forget the sentiment that my mother imparted while she crossed over. "I may live alone but I will never be alone," were the words I heard or, rather, could feel being said to me. In that instant, I knew my mother's spirit had already crossed to the other side, and a peace like no other filled me. I don't have a name for that feeling, or for the words that I heard, or felt.

But something else happened during my mother's viewing which happened seconds after saying my farewell to her. I felt a cold chill run down my spine and would learn that Raeford Manor Rest Home mysteriously caught on fire.

My mother did not want to be buried next to my father and nor could I blame her. At her request, she was buried in White Oak, NC next to her mother, where she could rest in peace.

CHAPTER 17
Keys to a New Life

My father had seen more than he cared to in his life, and before going blind he compiled a box of his most prized possessions and sent them to me in Florida, knowing better than anyone that he wouldn't be taking them with him when he left this world.

Most of the items were antiques that I was fond of as a child, and he had kept my collection of childhood books. I was in my attic retrieving one of those books a few years after his death when I found a box that had been previously overlooked. I brought it downstairs, and opened it immediately.

Inside the cardboard box was a wooden box wrapped in old newspaper. I lifted the top and a familiar presence that I had not felt since childhood surrounded me. The crystal doorknob that I stared at for so long as a child now stared right back at me, no longer attached to the basement door. The doorknob lay atop an assortment of old skeleton keys. I didn't know what doors each of them opened, but one was unmistakable.

I knew that I finally held the key to my past, and it could no longer control me.

I don't claim to have psychic abilities but I know I can read signs from the other world, signs that most people overlook. But after growing up in that house on West Prospect

Avenue, I have no doubt that another dimension exists. And I don't care whether anyone else shares my beliefs, because I believe in myself. I have become extremely spiritual as the years have gone by.

"If you can see it then you can be it," is one of my favorite sayings. I can tell you that money and material things are helpful in this world but you can't take them with you to the next. It is not what you accumulate that will decide your fate in the afterworld. It's what you give back to make this world better. .

And while some folks will dismiss my story as a made-up tale, or the rantings of a lunatic, I know that some people out there will relate perfectly to my experiences. This story is for them, to let them know they are not alone.

I believe my father still resides in the home he created, and is one of the ghosts that shares the house with Ms. Adams. And if that's the case, better her than me.

LAST WORDS

The house still stands on West Prospect Avenue in Raeford, N.C., and has seen numerous owners since my father sold it in the 1980s.

No one has stayed for more than three years.

The current owner, Nettie Adams, is the first occupant since me to acknowledge the ghosts that live there and the otherworldly occurrences that have come to be part of her "normal" existence.

There's that word again, normal. Who's to decide what it is?

Ms. Adams and I have never met, but I believe we have a connection in my father. He used to say that the funeral home would always belong to him because he's the one who created it.

Even though it was a house of secrets, nightmares and death, it was also the only home I knew, and it made me who I am today.

ACKNOWLEDGEMENTS

So many people, with their influence, skills, support and expertise, made this book possible, and I am forever grateful to those who made my vision a reality. My heartfelt appreciation goes out to:

Maria Satchell for her graphic design mastery
Mandy Miles for her astounding editing skills
Diane Bowers for her helpful input
Jeffrey Bonior for his proofreading willingness
Michelle McNab Herman for her mentoring, support and guidance
Eva and David Horne for years of unconditional love and guidance
Manny Anillo for beautiful smiles and encouragement on this book
Sandra Berrisko for believing I could be the teacher I always wanted to be
Jean Holland, my very first teacher
Jean Lentz, cousin and guide through some of my darkest hours
Chance, the son who has made me proud to be a mother
The friends and relatives I am blessed to have:
Kenneth and Betty Smith, Ron and Hannah Schmidt,
Johnny Brennan, Pam and David Horne, Sonia Delgaldo,
Rocking Robbie, Mike Cohen, Tim Choate,
The entire Crowder family,
Keith Floyd, Amy Hemmends, Selena Livingston,
Debbie Gordon, Colleen Martinez,
"The Energizer Bunny," and my dog, Flashy.

Thanks also to all my former teachers at Hoke County High School, and to the professors and administrators of the Title 5 Program and the Broward College 21st Century Education Program
Thanks to my fellow Friends of Bill W.
Special thanks to the people of Raeford, N.C.
Thanks to my Creator

And in loving memory of my parents,
James C. and LaRue Brennan Lentz.

What Everyone Should Know About Autism

Autism affects the way a child perceives the world, making communication and social interaction extremely difficult. Symptoms of autism vary greatly among those affected, with some children exhibiting repetitive behavior, while others will not speak or will demonstrate intense, almost obsessive, interests.

Two children of the same age may have the same diagnosis, but will seem very different from each other in their behavior, communication and interaction.

It has been said, "If you know one person with autism; you know one person with autism."

Such is the individuality of the symptoms, which typically last throughout a person's lifetime. A mildly affected person might seem merely quirky and lead a typical life. A severely affected person might be unable to speak or care for himself.

Early intervention can make extraordinary differences in a child's development. An autistic person's skills and capabilities may increase throughout their life.

Treatment for autism is an intensive, comprehensive undertaking that involves the child's entire family and a team of professionals.

There is currently no known cause of or cure for autism, and its prevalence is increasing at an alarming rate.

Please have compassion for individuals who live with autism not only for them but for their family.

Author's Note:
Ina Lentz Griesbeck is a teacher who specializes in severely emotionally disabled students, many of whom are autistic.
A portion of the proceeds from this book will be used to help fund research and raise awareness of this baffling neurological condition.